collector's guide to
CIGARETTE *Lighters*

James Flanagan

COLLECTOR BOOKS

A Division of Schroeder Publishing Co., Inc.

Cover design by Beth Summers
Book design by Karen Geary

Searching For A Publisher?

We are always looking for knowledgeable people considered to be experts within their fields. If you feel that there is a real need for a book on your collectible subject and have a large comprehensive collection, contact Collector Books.

Collector Books
P.O. Box 3009
Paducah, KY 42002-3009

www.collectorbooks.com

Copyright © 1995 by James Flanagan

— DEDICATION —

To my best friend and loving wife, Patricia who really co-authored this book. Her help, patience, understanding, and encouragement made this project possible.

— ON THE COVER —

Chromium lift arm pocket lighter with mother-of-pearl inlay. Made in Occupied Japan. Circa 1948. $60.00–85.00.

Sterling silver pocket lighter made by D.P.R. in Germany. Circa early 1930's. $50.00–75.00.

Brass lighter with ivory floral decoration. Made by Pigeon. Circa early 1960's. $10.00–20.00.

Brass elephant lift arm table lighter. Body is painted metal. Circa mid-1930's. $25.00–40.00.

Brass and painted enamel table lighters made by Evans. Circa 1934. $15.00–35.00 each.

— ACKNOWLEDGMENTS —

— To my wonderful children, Teresa, Lisa, and Jimmy for spending countless hours with me in the search of those perfect lighters for my collection.

— To Judy Reilly for the many hours spent photographing my collection so beautifully.

— To Melvin Flanagan, my father for finding so many unique and interesting lighters for my collection.

— To all the friends I have made at antique shows, shops, and lighter collector clubs.

— Thanks very much to all of you.

— CONTENTS —

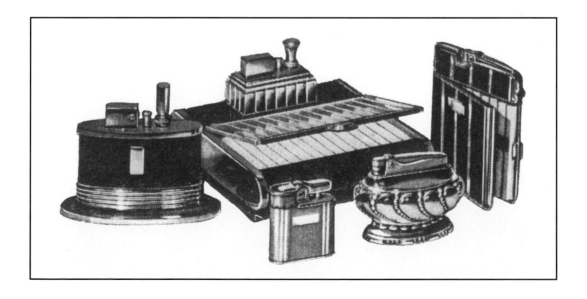

— INTRODUCTION —

From as far back as I can remember there have always been cigarette lighters in one form or another. There were pocket lighters, table lighters, cigarette lighter case combinations, and beautifully crafted sets in various sizes, shapes, and finishes. We also cannot forget the wonderful accessories that were crafted to go along with these lighters such as ashtrays, cigarette holders, smoking stands, etc.

This was not always the case though, early on the only thing that was available for lighting your smoking tobacco was a match carried in a box or match safe. At the turn of the century match safes were losing their appeal and the smoker was looking for a more convenient way to light their cigarettes, cigars, and pipe tobacco. So with someone's perseverance and imagination the self-contained pocket lighter was invented.

Around the time of the First World War the pocket lighter won its popularity by being easily carried and easy to use. As time went on more companies in the United States and abroad started manufacturing these wonderful items. From the simplest lighter that used fluid, flint, and a wick to the ones that used a more complicated mechanism like the "Capitol" lighter (pictured in plate #474 of this book), the making of the lighter

soon became an art form. There were striker type, touch tip, even lighters that used batteries or electricity to activate a heating element or coil and in the 1950's butane gas was introduced.

Today the popularity and acceptance of cigarette smoking has greatly diminished. Gone are the stylish, built-to-last lighters of years past. Only a handful of companies still make them well today. In our society the most popular lighters are the disposable butane ones that are made of different colored plastic.

Even though smoking is slowly becoming a thing of the past the same cannot be said about the collecting of lighters and related accessories. I first started collecting lighters in the early 1970's. At that time they were easy to find and relatively inexpensive, but with the growing interest in this type of collecting it is now much more challenging to find these treasures. There is help though! Many lighter clubs have been formed in the United States and abroad along with a cigarette lighter museum in Holland.

As you will find in the contents of this book there is something that would appeal to just about anyone. I hope you will enjoy a look back in time as you thumb through the pages of this publication.

— ADVERTISING —

Plate 1 • Chromium butane pocket lighters on a cardboard display by Bentley. Circa mid-1950's. 1½" H., 2" W. $20.00–30.00 each.

Plate 3 • Salem promotional pocket lighter with box, in chromium made by Zippo, regular size. Circa 1991. 2¼" H., 1½" W. $20.00–30.00.

Plate 4 • Salem promotional pocket lighter with box, in chromium made by Zippo, slim model. Circa 1991. 2¼" H., 1¼" W. $20.00–30.00.

Plate 2 • Chromium sports model butane pocket lighters on cardboard display by Bentley. Circa late 1950's. 1½" H., 2" W. $20.00–30.00 each.

Plate 5 • 1932 replica of chromium Zippo pocket lighter in a gift box. Circa 1988. 2½" H., 1½" W. $25.00–35.00.

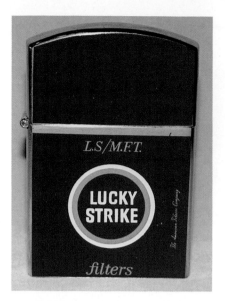

Plate 6 • Large Lucky Strike chromium and painted table lighter made in Japan. Circa late 1950's. 4⅜" H., 3" W. $30.00–40.00.

Plate 7 • Butane lighter in holder. "Denver Police Union" printed on holder made by Bic Pen Corp. Circa 1978. 3⅝" H., 2" W. $5.00–15.00.

Plate 8 • Brass pocket lighter with the "Fraternal Order Of Eagle" on the front made by Hurricane. Circa 1940's. 2¼" H., 1½" W. $20.00–30.00.

Plate 9 • Marlboro butane promotional pocket lighter in black. This lighter also available in yellow and red. Circa 1993. 2⅞" H., ½" W. $15.00–20.00.

Plate 10 • (a) Metal bottle shaped lighter painted red with an ad for Lutz Lounge made in Canada. Circa mid-1950's. 3¼" H., ½" Dia. $15.00–20.00. (b) Coor's beer plastic bowling pin. Made by KEM. Circa early 1950's. 2⅞" H.; ⅞" Dia. $20.00–25.00. (c) Guinness metal beer bottle. Made in Ireland. Circa mid-1960's. 2½" H., ¾" Dia. $15.00–20.00.

Plate 13 • Red Bakelite oil drum with an ad for Dodge Trucks. Circa 1940's. 3" H., 1¾" base Dia. $15.00–30.00.

Plate 14 • "Willie, the Kool Penguin" table lighter made of painted metal. Circa mid-1930's. 4" H., 1½" base Dia. $100.00–125.00.

Plate 11 • "Venetian" slim chromium pocket lighter by Zippo. Circa 1992. 2¼" H., 1¼" W. $20.00–30.00.

Plate 15 • Alpine and Philip Morris cigarette advertising pocket lighters made in Japan. Circa 1960's. Both 2" H., 1⅜" W. $15.00–20.00 each.

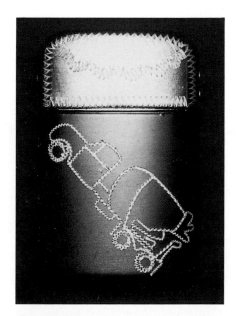

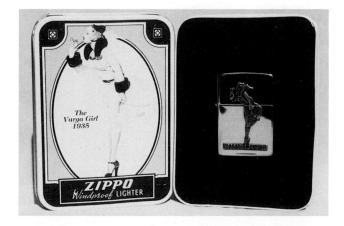

Plate 12 • "Typhoon" pocket lighter by Ronson with an engraving of a concrete truck done by hand. Circa mid-1960's. 2¼" H., 1½" W. $20.00–30.00.

Plate 16 • 1935 Varga Girl in pewter on a chromium finish Zippo lighter in a tin gift box. Circa 1993. 2¼" H., 1½" W. $40.00–50.00.

Plate 17 • Zippo anniversary series 1932–1992 chromium pocket lighters with tin gift box. Also came with six lapel pins. Circa 1993. 2¼" H., 1½" W. $95.00–120.00 for the set.

Plate 18 • Rosen-Nesor pocket lighter with "Lake Shore Club of Chicago" and emblem of the club on it, with box. Circa 1950's. 1¾" H., 2⅛" W. $15.00–25.00.

Plate 19 • Chromium and enamel painted pocket lighters. (a) Ad for a bank in Denver, Colorado. (b) Public Service of Oklahoma. (c) Winston cigarettes. All made in Japan. All circa 1960's. 1¾" H., 2⅛" W. $10.00–20.00 each.

Plate 20 • Metal oil drum for ZEP cleaner. Circa 1950's. 2¼" H., 1¼" Dia. $15.00–25.00.

Plate 21 • Brass table lighter with a pull chain mechanism. Has an eagle on top of the world with a banner saying "GMAC Plan." Circa 1935. 3¼" H., 2⅛" Dia. at base. $25.00–40.00.

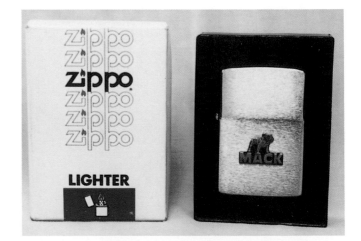

Plate 22 • Chromium promotional pocket lighter for Mack Truck by Zippo in a gift box. Circa 1976. 2¼" H., 1½" W. $25.00–35.00.

Plate 23 • Marlboro cigarettes promotional brass lighter by Zippo in a gift box. Circa 1991. 2¼" H., 1½" W. $25.00–35.00.

Plate 24 • Camel promotional cigarette lighter in a gift box by Zippo. Circa 1993. 2¼" H., 1½" W. $25.00–35.00.

Plate 25 • Bottle pocket lighters. (a) "Black & White." 2½" H., ¾" Dia. (b) Johnny Walker. 2⅜" H., ⅝" Dia. (c) VAT 69. 2¼" H., ¾" Dia. All circa early 1960's. $15.00–25.00 each.

Plate 26 • Glass bottles with metal caps. (a) Tribune Vermouth. Circa late 1950's. 5¼" H., 1⅜" Dia. $15.00–25.00. (b) Canadian Ale. Circa late 1950's. 5" H., 1⅛" Dia. $15.00–25.00.

Plate 27 • Plastic Coca-Cola bottles with metal caps. Could be used as pocket or table lighters. Circa 1953. 2½" H., ¾" Dia. $25.00–40.00 each.

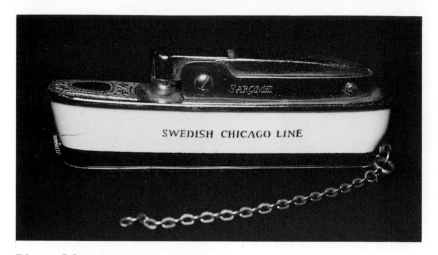

Plate 28 • Small table or pocket lighter of a ship for "Swedish Chicago Line" in chromium and paint by Sarome. Circa mid-1960's. 1⅛" H., 3¼" W. $20.00–30.00.

Plate 29 • Brushed chromium pocket lighter with old concrete mixer truck. Made for Walt Flanagan & Co. by Zippo. Circa 1986. 2¼" H., 1½" W. $25.00–35.00.

Plate 30 • Advertising lighter for Walt Flanagan & Co. Concrete. Made of brushed chromium by Rite Point, circa 1960. 2¼" H., 1½" W. $25.00–35.00.

Plate 31 • 1932 replica lighter with a service kit containing fluid, flint, cleaning brush, and tweezers in a gift box made by Zippo. Circa 1990. 2¼" H., 1½" W. $25.00–35.00.

Plate 32 • Chromium 60th (1932–1992) anniversary pocket lighter in a tin gift box made by Zippo. Circa 1992. $30.00–40.00.

Plate 33 • Spark plug lighter in chromium and paint by Bosch of Germany. Circa 1975. 3¼" H., ⅞" Dia. $25.00–40.00.

Plate 34 • International Lighter Collectors Seventh Annual Convention brass lighter by Zippo with a wooden box. Circa 1993. 2¼" H., 1½" W. $30.00–40.00.

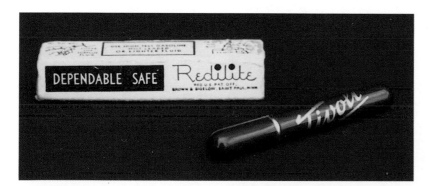

Plate 35 • Tube style painted blue enamel lighter for Tivoli Beer with box. This lighter used a genuine asbestos wick. Made by Redilite. Circa late 1940's. 3" H., ⅜" Dia. $30.00–45.00.

Plate 36 • Lucky Strike promotional lapel pin made of metal with baked enamel paint. Circa 1992. 1" H., 1⅛" W. $10.00–15.00.

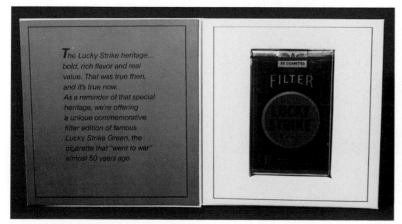

Plate 37 • Lucky Strike promotional cigarettes in a souvenir box. This is how they were packaged in 1940. Circa 1992. 3¼" H., 2⅛" W. $20.00–30.00.

Plate 38 • Lucky Strike promotional ceramic coffee cup. Circa 1992. 3¾" H., 5" W. $10.00–15.00.

Plate 39 • Advertisement for Lucky Strike cigarettes from a magazine. Picture mounted in glass with a brass frame. Circa late 1930's. 12" H., 8¼" W. $10.00–20.00.

Plate 40 • Lucky Strike promotional chromium pocket lighter in a gift box made by Zippo. Circa 1992. 2¼" H., 1½" W. $25.00–40.00.

— ANIMALS —

Plate 41 • Dinosaur chromium butane table lighter made in Japan. Circa 1988. 4¾" H., 4" W. $20.00–30.00.

Plate 43 • Imperial bronze dachshund strike type table lighter by Ronson. (Tail is the striker.) Circa 1940. 4" H., 9" W. $175.00–250.00.

Plate 42 • Chromium butane table lighter of a horse made in Japan. Circa 1988. 7" H., 4½" W. $20.00–30.00.

Plate 44 • Metal table lighters. (a) Elephant. Circa 1935. 2¼" H., 2½" W. $25.00–40.00. (b) Bear. Circa 1935. 2" H., 2½" W. $35.00–50.00 each.

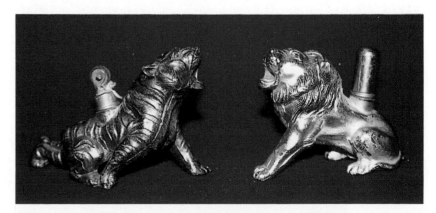

Plate 45 • (a) Metal tiger-shaped table lighter. Circa 1935. 1¾" H., 2⅜" W. $25.00–40.00. (b) Silverplated lion table lighter. Circa 1935. 1¾" H., 2⅜" W. $40.00–70.00.

Plate 46 • Brass dog with front paws on a fence looking at a book. (Book is the lighter.) Made in Occupied Japan. Circa 1948. 2⅝" H., 2⅜" W. $80.00–120.00.

Plate 47 • Brass horse head table lighter with leather reins. This lighter is lit when the reins are pulled back. Circa late 1940's. 4¾" H., 3¾" W. $50.00–75.00.

Plate 48 • Metal painted camel with a lift arm lighter. Circa mid-1930's. 2½" H., 4¾" W. $35.00–45.00.

Plate 49 • Brass lift arm table lighter. The body of the elephant is painted metal. Circa mid-1930's. 3⅜" H., 4⅞" W. $30.00–40.00.

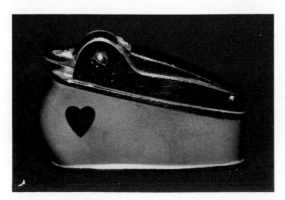

Plate 50 • Bird-shaped pocket lighter in brushed and smooth chromium finish. Circa 1958. 1½" H., 2⅛" W. $20.00–30.00.

Plate 51 • Chromium elephant strike type table lighter by Ronson. (Note the tusks are missing.) Circa 1935. 5" H., 3¾" W. $75.00–150.00.

Plate 52 • Chromium "Houn' Dog" strike type table lighter by Ronson. Circa 1934. 4½" H., 4" W. $50.00–100.00.

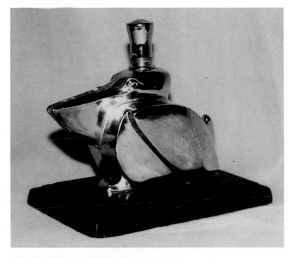

Plate 53 • Chromium swan table lighter made in Japan. Circa early 1960's. 3" H., 3¾" W. $10.00–20.00.

Plate 54 • "Dodo Bird" chromium strike type table lighter by Ronson. Circa 1934. 3½" H., 4" W. $75.00–110.00.

Plate 55 • Metal tiger table lighters. Both made in Japan. Circa 1935. (a) 2⅛" H., 3" W. $25.00–40.00. (b) 2⅞" H., 2⅛" W. $50.00–75.00.

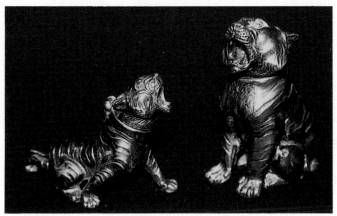

Plate 56 • Painted ceramic horse table lighter made in Japan. Circa 1955. 5½" H., 5½" W. $15.00–25.00.

Plate 57 • Brass elephant table lighter made in Austria. "Pat. April 2, 1912." Circa 1913. 3" H., 3½" W. $90.00–115.00.

Plate 58 • Silver and brass lion table lighter. "Patent April 2, 1912." Circa 1913. 2¾" H., 2" W. $75.00–125.00.

Plate 59 • Black metal butane pocket lighter with a silver owl on the front. Made by Ronson. Circa mid-1960's. 3" H., 1" Dia. $10.00–25.00.

Plate 60 • Gold and silverplated penguin table lighter. Circa 1960. 2" H., ⅞" Dia. $40.00–70.00.

Plate 61 • Metal table lighter with a poodle dog for a handle. Circa mid-1960's. 2¾" H., 2" Dia. $10.00–25.00.

— ART DECO —

Plate 62, 63 • Chromium and glass airplane smoke stand. This stand, shown at different angles, contains a pipe holder, tobacco holder, and ashtray. The plane's interior and the glass base have lights for illumination during use at night. Circa mid-1930's. 37½" H., 10" Dia. at base. $400.00–550.00 each.

Plate 64 • "Grecian" touch tip table lighter in chromium and tortoise enamel. Circa post-World War II. 3⅞" H., 2⅝" Dia. at base. $75.00–100.00.

Plate 65 • "Classic" chromium and tortoise enamel touch tip table lighter by Ronson. Circa 1938. 3⅝" H., 3¾" W. $150.00–200.00.

Plate 66 • "Octette" touch tip table lighter in chromium and black enamel by Ronson. Circa post-World War II. 3½" H., 3¾" W. $100.00–125.00.

Plate 67 • The "Electro-Match" table lighter in black plastic with gold trim made by Korex Co. Circa 1950's. 5¾" H., 4½" Dia. $10.00–25.00.

Plate 68 • Chromium nude female with Bakelite ashtray. Made by Harry Davis Molding Co. Circa 1935. 5" H., 6¾" Dia. $30.00–45.00.

Plate 69, 70 • Bartender table lighters in chromium and walnut enamel. Made by Ronson, circa 1936. (a) Touch tip lighter with cigarette compartments on each end. 7" H., 6" W. $1,400.00–2,000.00. (b) Strike type lighter with cigarette holder in the front that tips out. 6⅞" H., 5⅜" W. $1,200.00–1,800.00.

Plate 71 • Junior Bartender touch tip table lighter in chromium and walnut enamel by Ronson. Circa 1937. 7½" H., 4¼" W. $800.00–1,200.00.

Plate 72 • Brass art deco lady ashtray. The base of the ashtray looks like a book. Circa 1930's. 8" H., 6" W. $75.00–100.00.

— BEYOND THE ORDINARY —

Plate 73 • LEKTRoLITE cylinder pocket lighter with box, fluid, and instructions. Circa late 1930's. 2⅝" H., ½" Dia. $30.00–45.00.

Plate 74 • Chromium and leather pocket lighter/flashlight by Aurora. Circa 1960. 2" H., 2½" W. $25.00–35.00.

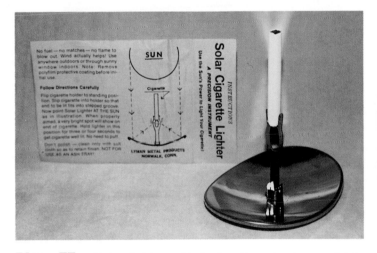

Plate 75 • Solar lighter with instructions by Lyman Meta Products. Circa 1980's. 2¾" H., 4" W. $5.00–10.00.

Plate 76 • Electric table lighter, glass base with a jockey on a horse. Circa mid-1930's. 3½" H., 2⅜" Dia. $40.00–60.00.

Plate 77 • Ceramic "Gremlin" electric lighter by Aircraft Novelty Co. Sold new for $3.95. Circa mid-1930's. 4¼" H., 4" W. $75.00–100.00.

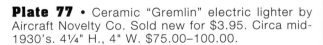

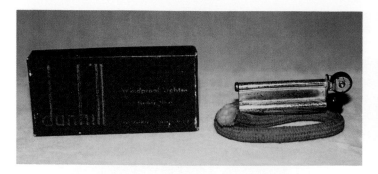

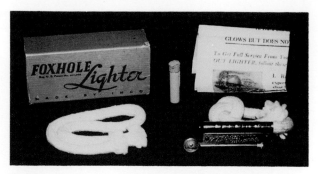

Plate 78 • Chromium pocket lighter with box, instructions, and spare wick made by Dunhill. Circa early 1940's. 2¼" H., ¾" W. $90.00–120.00.

Plate 79 • Chromium foxhole pocket lighter with box, instructions, flint, and spare wick by IMACO. Circa early 1940's. 2⅝" H., ¾" W. $40.00–60.00.

Plate 80 • (a) Metal striker type pocket lighter. Circa mid-1930's. 1⅞" H., 1⅛" W. $20.00– 40.00. (b) Bakelite striker type pocket lighter. Circa late 1930's. 1⅞" H., 1⅛" W. $15.00–35.00. (c) Metal book-shaped striker lighter. Circa mid-1930's. 1⅞" H., 1⅛" W. $20.00–40.00.

Plate 81 • Metal striker style pocket lighter. Circa late 1930's. 2½" H., 1½" W. $20.00–40.00.

Plate 82 • Chromium pocket lighter with box, by New Method Mfg. Co. Circa early 1930's. 2" H., 1⅛" W. $40.00–50.00.

Plate 83 • Battery and butane-operated telegraph style table lighter. Made of plastic, brass, and wood from Japan. Circa mid-1950's. 3¾" H., 6" W. $30.00–50.00.

Plate 84 • Chromium electric table lighter by Mico. Circa mid-1930's. 3¾" H., 2¼" W. $30.00–50.00.

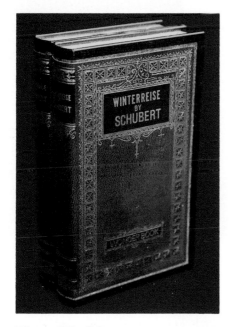

Plate 85, 86 • Book style table lighter made of plastic uses batteries and butane. Books separate to reveal lighter. Circa mid-1950's. 5½" H., 3¼" W. $25.00–35.00 each.

Plate 87 • Chromium pocket lighter/ flashlight with box and instructions. Battery operated. Made by Magna. Circa early 1950's. 2¼" H., 2" W. $35.00–50.00.

Plate 88 • Electric telephone table lighter with built-in clock and ashtrays on each side. Made of metal with painted enamel finish. Circa late 1930's. 3½" H., 1¼" W. $75.00–100.00.

Plate 89 • Chromium pocket lighter/flashlight. Battery operated. Made in Japan. 2⅞" H., 1½" W. $20.00–30.00.

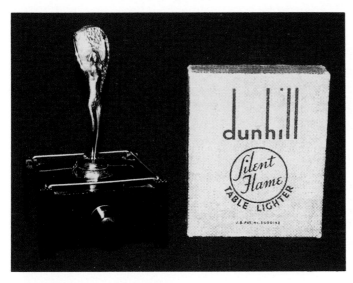

Plate 90 • Chromium nude on a plastic base. Operated on batteries and fluid. Made by Dunhill. Circa 1935. 5" H., 3" W. $70.00–100.00.

Plate 91 • Large table "Jump Spark" cigar lighter made of wood and metal. This lighter operated on batteries, fluid, and wick. Made by Midland. Circa 1920. 15" H., 7¼" W. $350.00–500.00.

Plate 92 • Painted metal electric table lighter. Circa mid-1930's. 2⅛" H., 2⅜" Dia. at base. $30.00–45.00.

Plate 93 • "Gloria" table lighter made of plastic and brass. Operated with batteries and butane. Circa mid-1960's. 7¼" H., 4¼" Dia. at base. $30.00–50.00.

Plate 94 • Statue of Liberty table lighter. Operated with batteries and butane. Circa mid-1950's. 7½" H., 3½" W. $90.00–115.00.

Plate 95 • "Rony" table lighter made of plastic and metal. Operated with batteries and butane. Circa mid-1960's. 11" H., 4⅜" Dia. at base. $40.00–60.00.

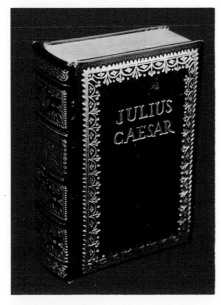

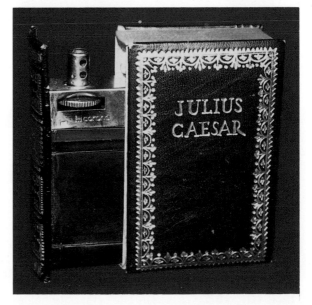

Plate 96, 97 • Book-style table lighter. Book spine pulls open for lighting. Uses batteries and butane. Circa mid-1950's. 4" H., 2¾" W. $40.00–60.00 each.

Plate 98 • Electric brass table lighter of a woman's head. The heating element is in the mouth. Circa 1920's. 7½" H., 4¼" W. $170.00–230.00.

Plate 99 • Chromium and painted metal table lighter shaped like kerosene heater. Operates with batteries and butane. Circa mid-1960's. 5¾" H., 3⅞" W. $30.00–50.00.

Plate 100 • Nude electric brass table lighter. Circa 1925. 6½" H., 3" W. at base. $90.00–110.00.

Plate 101, 102 • "Press-A-Lite" cigarette holder and lighter made of metal and Bakelite. Has hardware to mount on a car steering column. Shown with box and instructions. Circa late 1940's. 2⅝" H., 3⅝" W. $75.00–100.00.

Plate 103 • Large table size rocket ship made of metal and gold-colored plastic. Operated with batteries and butane. Circa 1965. 8½" H., 4¼" Dia. at base. $50.00–80.00.

— CHEESECAKE —

Plate 104 • Nude silverplated table lighter on a marble base. Circa 1912. 7" H., 5½" W. $150.00–200.00.

Plate 105 • Chromium nude with Bakelite ashtray made by Harry Davis Molding Co. Circa 1935. 5" H., 6¾" Dia. $40.00–60.00.

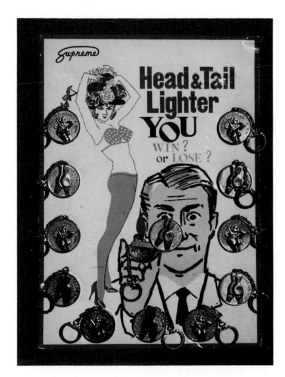

Plate 106, 107 • "Head & Tail" pocket lighter made of metal with a key chain by Supreme. (Lighters shown close-up and on cardboard display.) Circa late 1950's. 1½" Dia. $25.00–35.00 each.

Plate 108 • "Miss Cutie" table lighter shown with box. Made of gold-tone plastic, by Negbaur. Circa mid-1950's. 4¾" H., 1½" Dia. at base. $25.00–50.00.

Plate 109 • Nude chromium table lighter. Both circa 1988. (a) 3" H., 1⅞" W. $15.00–30.00. (b) 3" H., 1⅝" W. $15.00–30.00.

Plate 110 • Photos of females inside "Vu-Lighters." Made of clear plastic and chromium by Scripto. Both circa late 1950's. 2¾" H., 1½" W. $25.00–40.00 each.

Plate 112 • Pocket "Vu-Lighter" has metal box with instructions and guarantee. Made by Scripto. Circa late 1950's. 2¾" H., 1½" W. $40.00–50.00.

Plate 111 • Chromium nude with a basket. Circa 1950. 6" H., 2⅜" Dia. at base. $15.00–30.00.

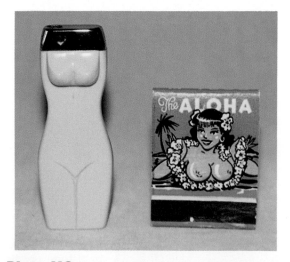

Plate 113 • (a) Plastic female butane pocket lighter. Circa 1985. 2⅞" H., 1" W. $15.00–20.00. (b) Matches from a club in Hawaii. Circa mid-1950's. 2" H., 1½" W. $10.00–15.00.

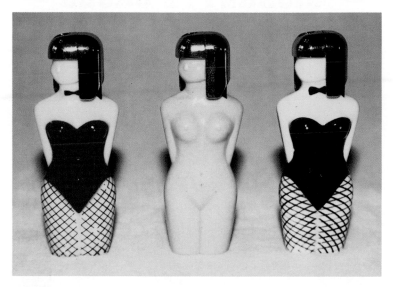

Plate 114 • Painted plastic female butane pocket lighter. Circa 1988. 3" H., 1⅛" W. $15.00–20.00 each.

Plate 115 • Pin-up pocket lighters in chromium, made by Supreme. Circa 1950's. 2" H., 1⅝" W. $25.00–30.00 each.

— CIGARETTE CASES —

Plate 116 • Chromium and black enamel "Mastercase" cigarette lighter/case by Ronson. Circa 1933. 4¾" H., 2½" W. $40.00–60.00.

Plate 117 • Brass with black and white enamel cigarette lighter/case by Marathon. Circa mid-1930's. 4¼" H., 2⅝" W. $35.00–55.00.

Plate 118 • "Mastercase" in chromium and tortoise enamel cigarette lighter/case by Ronson. Circa 1933. 4⅜" H., 2½" W. $40.00–60.00.

Plate 119 • Chromium "Mastercase" cigarette lighter/case by Ronson. Circa 1933. 4⅜" H., 2⅝" W. $25.00–50.00.

Plate 120 • Cigarette lighter/case in chromium and black enamel made by Evans. Circa late 1930's. 4¼" H., 2½" W. $30.00–50.00.

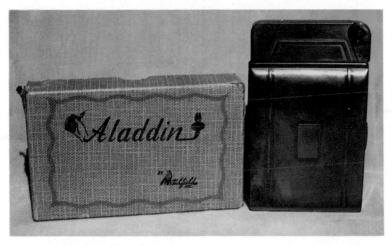

Plate 121 • Goldplated cigarette lighter/case with gift box. When the case is closed, the lighter automatically lights. Made by Aladdin. Circa early 1930's. 4⅞" H., 2⅞" W. $50.00–60.00.

Plate 122 • Cigarette case covered with leopard skin. Circa mid-1930's. 5½" H., 5½" W. $30.00–45.00.

Plate 123 • Chromium cigarette case with a watch made by Evans. Circa 1935. 4⅜" H., 3⅛" W. $100.00–150.00.

Plate 124 • Chromium and black "Twentycase" with gift box by Ronson. Circa 1935. 4¼" H., 3" W. $75.00–100.00.

Plate 125 • Brass and tortoise enamel cigarette lighter/case in a gift box. Made by Elgin American. Circa 1940's. 3¼" H., 4⅞" W. $70.00–90.00.

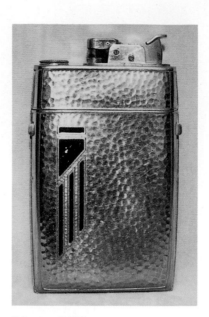

Plate 126 • Chromium cigarette lighter/case by Evans. Circa early 1950's. 5¾" H., 3¼" W. $70.00–90.00.

Plate 127 • Chromium and black enamel cigarette lighter/case by Evans. Circa early 1930's. 4¼" H., 2½" W. $60.00–80.00.

Plate 128 • Chromium and black enamel cigarette lighter/case by Evans. Circa early 1950's. 4¾" H., 2½" W. $50.00–70.00.

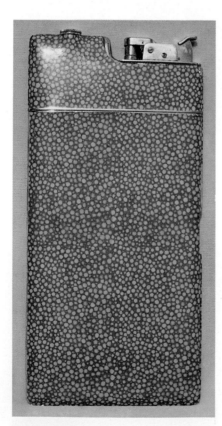

Plate 129 • Enameled finish cigarette lighter/case by Evans. Circa mid-1930's. 6¾" H., 3¼" W. $60.00–80.00.

Plate 130 • The "Pal" cigarette lighter/case by Ronson. Circa 1941. 4⅛" H., 2" W. $40.00–60.00.

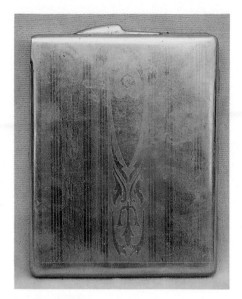

Plate 131 • Chromium cigarette case by Taico. Circa 1921. 2⅞" H., 3⅞" W. $25.00–40.00.

Plate 132 • Chromium cigarette case. "Pat. Mar. 2, 1926," by Iymco Esector. Circa 1927. 3¾" H., 3¼" W. $30.00–50.00.

Plate 133 • Brass cigarette case with built-in watch. Circa mid-1930's. 3" H., 3¼" W. $100.00–125.00.

Plate 134 • Cigarette lighter/case in brass and two-toned enamel. Circa early 1950's. 4½" H., 3" W. $30.00–50.00.

Plate 135 • Chromium lift arm cigarette lighter/case made by Evans. Circa mid-1930's. 3⅛" H., 2½" W. $75.00–90.00.

— DECORATIVE —

Plate 136 • The "Decor" table lighter. The plastic cover can be removed to enable you to change the fabric to match your decor. Made by Ronson. Circa 1954. 2¾" H., 4¼" Dia. $25.00–40.00.

Plate 137 • Chromium butane airplane table lighter on a wood base. Circa early 1980's. 5" H., 12" W. $35.00–50.00.

Plate 138 • Chromium rose table lighter. The lighter is under the flower. Circa mid-1960's. 2½" H., 1⅝" Dia. at base. $20.00–35.00.

Plate 139 • Chromium bust of a knight on a tortoise-colored plastic cigarette box. Made by Negbaur. Circa early 1950's. 4⅛" H., 4" W. $30.00–50.00.

Plate 140 • Brass and marble-like plastic table lighter. Made by A.S.R. Circa 1950's. 2½" H., 3" W. $20.00–30.00.

Plate 141 • "Nordic" table lighter in glass and chromium, made by Ronson. Circa 1955. 3½" H., 3⅜" Dia. $25.00–40.00.

Plate 142 • Brass knight's helmet table lighter. Lights by pushing down on the visor. Circa mid-1950's. 5" H., 4" W. $10.00–20.00.

Plate 143 • Silverplated "Decanter" table lighter, made by Ronson. Circa 1936. 4½" H., 2½" Dia. $40.00–60.00.

Plate 146 • Chromium table lighter made by A.S.R. Circa 1950's. 2½" H., 3" W. $15.00–25.00.

Plate 144, 145 • Silverplated "Strikalite" table lighters made by W.B. Mfg. Co. Circa late 1940's. (a) 4" H., 1¾" Dia. at base. $25.00–40.00. (b) 3¾" H., 1½" Dia. at base. $25.00–40.00.

Plate 147 • Silverplated table lighter made by Evans. Circa 1950's. 3" H., 4¼" W. $30.00–45.00.

Plate 148 • Chromium table lighter made by Evans. Circa 1948. 4" H., 5" W. $30.00–50.00.

Plate 149 • Plastic table lighter on a wood base. Shaped like a knight's helmet. Circa 1960's. 5¾" H., 4" W. $5.00–15.00.

Plate 150, 151 • "Nordic" table lighters made by Ronson. Circa 1955. (a) Chromium and marble. 3½" H., 2⅞" Dia. $25.00–40.00. (b) Chromium and wood. 3½" H., 2¾" Dia. $25.00–40.00.

Plate 152 • Crystal butane table lighter made by Waterford in Ireland. Circa 1975. 3" H., 3½" Dia. $90.00–115.00.

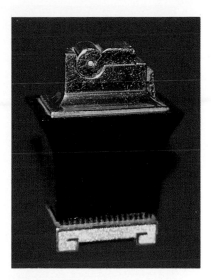

Plate 153 • Chromium table lighter by Evans. Circa 1934. 3" H., 2¼" W. $30.00–45.00.

Plate 154 • Brass and black plastic table lighter made by A.S.R. Circa early 1950's. 2¾" H., 1⅞" W. $20.00–30.00.

Plate 155 • Green Wedgwood-style table lighter made by Ronson. Circa 1962. 2¾" H., 2⅛" W. $50.00–70.00.

Plate 156 • Brass and painted enamel table lighters made by Evans. All circa 1934. All are 3½" H., 2¼" W. $25.00–45.00 each.

Plate 157 • "Diana" silverplated table lighter made by Ronson. Circa 1950. 2¼" H., 2¾" W. $30.00–40.00.

Plate 158 • Desk lighter/pen holder. When the pen holder is pushed down, the lighter is lit. Made in Japan. Circa 1953. 2¼" H., 3½" W. $50.00–70.00.

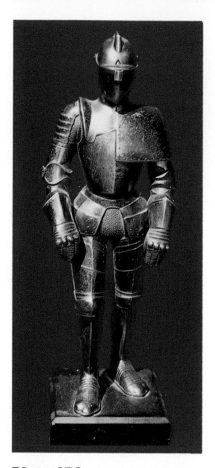

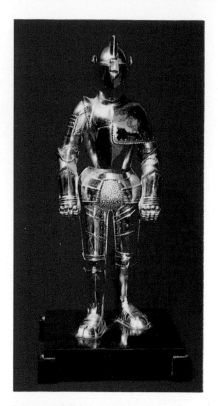

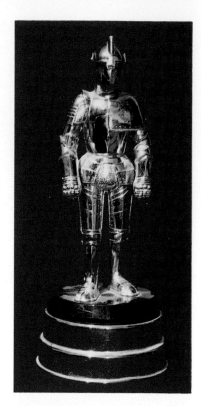

Plate 160 • Chromium knight on a plastic base. The lighter is in the helmet. Made by Thorens. Circa late 1940's. 6⅞" H., 3" W. $30.00–45.00.

Plate 159 • Large chromium knight table lighter. Lights by pushing button on helmet. Made by Hamilton. Circa late 1940's. 9½" H., 2⅞" W. $60.00–85.00.

Plate 161 • Chromium table lighter of a knight. When this lighter is picked up, the music box located in the base plays "The Bells of St. Mary." Made by Thorens. Circa early 1950's. 8" H., 3¾" Dia. at base. $40.00–65.00.

Plate 162 • Chromium butane table lighter of a knight on a horse. Circa 1988. 7" H., 6" W. $35.00–50.00.

Plate 163 • Chromium bust of a knight on a plastic base. The lighter is in the helmet. Made by Negbaur. Circa 1950's. 3" H., 3¾" W. $20.00–40.00.

Plate 164 • Knight table lighter. Metal striker type. Striker is in the helmet and is struck on the front of the base. Circa late 1930's. 9½" H., 3⅝" W. $80.00–110.00.

Plate 165 • Chromium table lighter on a plastic base. Bust of a knight design. Made by Hamilton. Circa early 1950's. 4½" H., 4" W. $25.00–40.00.

Plate 166 • Silverplated table lighter made in Japan. Circa late 1930's. 3¼" H., 1⅝" Dia. $30.00–45.00.

Plate 167 • "Mayfair" silverplated table lighter by Ronson. Circa 1936. 3" H., 1⅝" W. $15.00–25.00.

Plate 168 • Gold-toned brass apple table lighter made by Evans. Circa mid-1950's. 3" H., 2¼" Dia. $40.00–60.00.

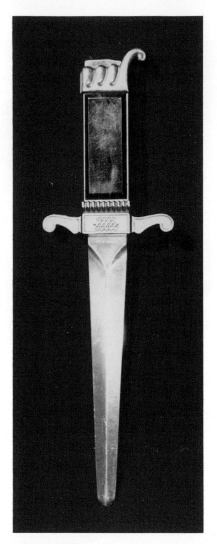

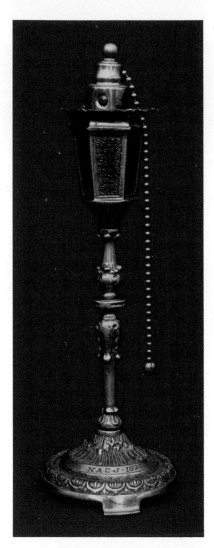

Plate 169 • Metal letter opener/lighter with plastic grips on the handle. Made by A.S.R. Circa 1950's. 9⅞" H., 2¾" W. $25.00–40.00.

Plate 170 • Brass lamp post table lighter. Lights when the chain is pulled. Circa 1929. 9½" H., 3" Dia. at base. $75.00–100.00.

Plate 171, 172 • Egg-shaped table lighters made by Evans. Circa mid-1950's. Both are 2½" H., 3" W. (a) Hand-painted egg. $60.00–75.00. (b) Brass egg. $40.00–60.00.

Plate 173 • Table lighter with three goldplated cherubs. Circa 1935. 7" H., 3⅛" Dia. at base. $25.00–50.00.

Plate 174 • Ceramic and brass candle-shaped table lighter. (Spare flint in flame.) Made by Giv-A-Gift Inc. Circa mid-1960's. 6¼" H., 3¼" Dia. $20.00–40.00.

Plate 175 • Plastic and glass ticker tape machine table lighter. Made in Japan. Circa late 1950's. 5¼" H., 3¼" Dia. $35.00–60.00.

— GUNS —

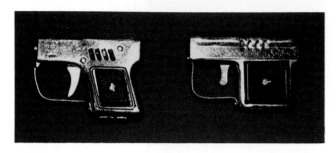

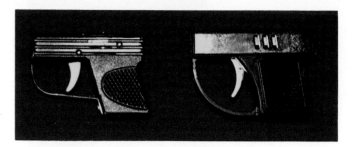

Plate 176 • Chromium pistol lighters with black plastic grips. Made in Japan. Both circa mid-1950's. (a) 1½"H., 2" W. $15.00–25.00. (b) 1⅜" H., 2" W. $15.00–25.00.

Plate 177 • Pistols made in Japan. Both circa mid-1950's. (a) All metal, painted black. 1½"H., 2⅛" W. $15.00–25.00. (b) Chromium with black plastic grips. 1⅝" H., 2¼" W. $15.00–30.00.

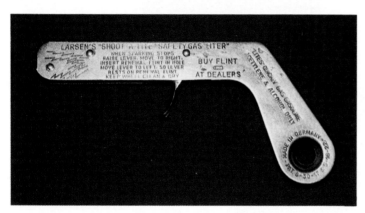

Plate 178 • Pistol-shaped spark maker used to light gas stoves, ovens, etc. Has the following markings –"Larsen's Shoot-A-Lite Safety Gas Liter." Made in Germany, Pat. 5-16-1922. Circa 1923. 3½" H., 6¼" W. $75.00–100.00.

Plate 179 • Chromium double-barrel pistol butane lighter. Made in Japan. Circa early 1980's. 3" H., 5½" W. $15.00–25.00.

Plate 180 • Chromium Beretta pistol butane table lighter. Circa 1988. 4¾" H., 6¼" W. $20.00–30.00.

Plate 181 • Chromium Thompson machine gun butane table lighter. Circa 1988. 3¾" H., 11¼" W. $35.00–60.00.

Plate 182 • Brass-plated Derringer gun table lighter. Made in Japan. Circa mid-1970's. 4¼" H., 8" W. $10.00–20.00.

Plate 183 • Brass cannon table lighter. Made in Japan. Circa 1938. 2½" H., 5½" W. $30.00–40.00.

Plate 184 • Brass cannon table lighter made by Negbaur. Circa 1939. 3⅛" H., 8" W. $50.00–75.00.

Plate 185 • Chromium pistol table lighter on a stand. Made in Occupied Japan. Circa 1949. 2½" H., 3½" W. $75.00–100.00.

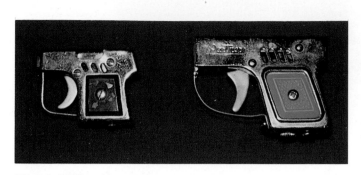

Plate 186 • Chromium pistols with plastic grips. Both were made in Japan. Circa mid-1950's. (a) 1⅜" H., 2" W. $20.00–30.00. (b) 1½" H., 2¼" W. $20.00–30.00.

Plate 187 • Chromium pistol with plastic grips on a stand. Made in Occupied Japan. Circa 1949. 2½" H., 3¾" W. $70.00–90.00.

Plate 188 • Chromium pistols with plastic grips. (a) Made in Occupied Japan. Circa 1949. 2" H., 2¾" W. $30.00–60.00. (b) Made in Japan. Circa mid-1950's. 2¼" H., 3" W. $50.00–70.00.

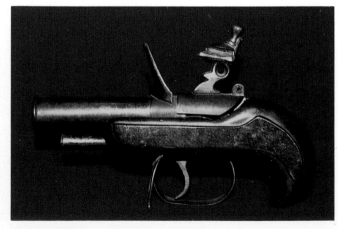

Plate 189 • Metal pistol lighter. (When the trigger is pulled, the top half of the gun opens to light the wick.) Made in Austria by Dandy. Circa early 1930's. 2¼" H., 3" W. $100.00–125.00.

Plate 190 • Brass dueling pistol table lighter. Made by Dunhill. Circa 1930. 4" H., 6¼" W. $225.00–300.00.

Plate 191 • Chromium pistol with black plastic grips on a stand. Made in Occupied Japan. Circa 1949. 2½" H., 3½" W. $70.00–90.00.

Plate 192 • Chromium and plastic Derringer gun on a plastic stand. Circa 1968. 3" H., 5¾" W. $15.00–30.00.

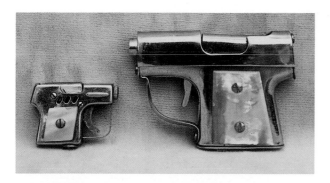

Plate 193 • Chromium pistols with mother-of-pearl handles. Both are Made in Occupied Japan. Circa 1949. (a) 1⅛" H., 1½" W. $40.00–60.00. (b) 2" H., 3" W. $70.00–90.00.

Plate 194 • Chromium pistols are Made in Occupied Japan. Circa 1949. (a) Plastic grips. 2¾" H., 3¾" W. $60.00–80.00. (b) Mother-of-pearl grips. 3" H., 3⅞" W. $70.00–90.00.

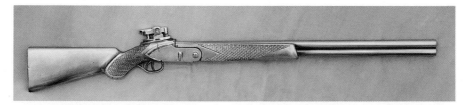

Plate 195 • Chromium double barrel shotgun butane table lighter. Circa early 1980's. 3" H., 20½" W. $30.00–50.00.

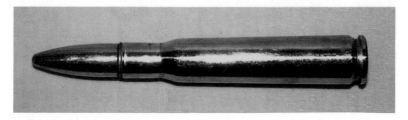

Plate 196 • Silver bullet table lighter. Circa early 1940's. 5⅜" H., ¾" Dia. $15.00–25.00.

— MINIATURES —

Plate 197 • Chromium lift arm lighter with a Japanese scene painted on. Made by Perky. Circa early 1950's. ⅞" H., ¾" W. $35.00–50.00.

Plate 198 • All chromium with mesh bands. Made in Occupied Japan. Circa 1949. (a) 1½" H., 1⅛" W. $30.00–50.00. (b) 1⅛" H., ⅞" W. $30.00–50.00. (c) ⅞" H., ¾" W. $35.00–50.00. (d) ¾" H., ¾" W. $35.00–50.00.

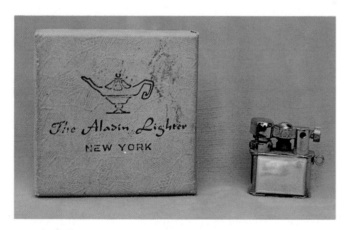

Plate 199 • Chromium lift arm lighter with mother-of-pearl band with gift box. Made by Aladin of New York. Circa mid-1950's. ⅞" H., ¾" W. $40.00–60.00.

Plate 200 • Both chromium lighters are made in Japan. Circa mid-1950's. (a) 1½" H., ⅞" W. $5.00–10.00. (b) 1" H., ⅝" W. $5.00–10.00.

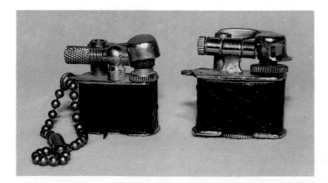

Plate 201 • Chromium lift arm lighters with leather bands. Both are Made in Occupied Japan. Circa 1948. (a) 1" H., 1" W. (b) 1⅛" H., ⅞" W. $30.00–45.00 each.

Plate 202 • (a) Chromium lift arm lighter with white leather band. Made in Japan. Circa mid-1950's. ⅞" H., ¾" W. $20.00–30.00. (b) Chromium lift arm with a female on the plastic band. Made in Japan. Circa mid-1950's. ⅞" H., ¾" W. $20.00–35.00.

Plate 203 • (a) Brass pocket lighter with key chain. Made by Pereline. Circa mid-1950's. 1¼" H., 1¼" W. $5.00–10.00. (b) Brass lighter with key chain. Made by Royal Star. Circa mid-1950's. 1¼" H., 1¼" W. $5.00–10.00.

Plate 204 • Chromium lift arm with metal band. Made in Occupied Japan. Circa 1948. 1⅝" H., 1⅛" W. $30.00–50.00.

Plate 205 • Both chromium lift arm table lighters with mother-of-pearl on the front and back. Made in Occupied Japan. Circa 1948. 1¼" H., 1⅜" W. at base. $35.00–45.00 each.

Plate 206 • Chromium lift arm lighter. Made in Occupied Japan. Circa 1948. (a) Has a unique flint wheel. ⅞" H., ⅞" W. $40.00–60.00. (b) ⅞" H., ⅞" W. $20.00–40.00.

Plate 207 • Chromium lift arm lighters with leather bands and attached key chain. Made in Occupied Japan. Circa 1948. (a) ⅞" H., ¾" W. (b) ⅞" H., ⅞" W. $20.00–40.00 each.

Plate 208 • Chromium and painted lift arm lighter with the state of Alaska on the front. Circa late 1950's. ⅞" H., ⅝" W. $20.00–35.00.

— NOVELTY —

Plate 209, 210 • Brass lamp with enamel painted shade table lighters. Circa 1950's. (a) Lighter operated by pushing the button on the base. 3½" H., 1¾" Dia. at base. $20.00–35.00. (b) Pull chain under the shade to light. 4¼" H., 1⅝" Dia. at base. $20.00–30.00.

Plate 211 • Plastic cigar-shaped lighter. Made by Negbaur. Circa 1955. 2½" H., ⅝" Dia. $20.00–30.00.

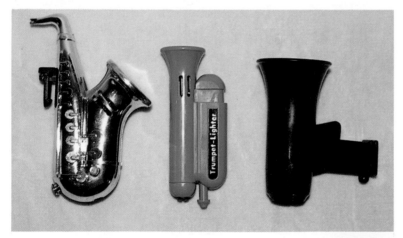

Plate 212 • Butane pocket lighters from Germany. All circa 1990. (a) Saxophone. 3½" H., 2" W. $15.00–25.00. (b) Trumpet. 3" H., 1¼" W. $15.00–25.00. (c) Megaphone. 2⅞" H., 2" W. $15.00–25.00.

Plate 213 • Butane pocket lighters from Germany. All circa 1990. (a) Lowenbrau beer can. 2⅜" H., ⅞" Dia. $15.00–25.00. (b) Wrench. 2⅞" H., 1¼" W. $15.00–25.00. (c) Electric drill. 2" H., 3" W. $15.00–25.00.

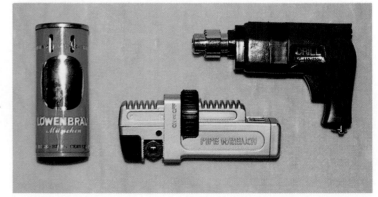

Plate 214 • Plastic butane pocket lighter that looks like a book of matches. Circa 1985. 1½" H., 2¼" W. $15.00–25.00.

Plate 215 • Ceramic Model T Ford table lighter. Circa 1964. 3¼" H., 4" W. $10.00–20.00.

Plate 216 • Butane pocket lighters from Germany. All circa 1990. (a) Jukebox that lights up and plays music when it is lit. 2¾" H., 1⅜" W. $15.00–25.00. (b) Sunglasses. 1" H., 3½" W. $15.00–25.00. (c) Cassette tape. 1½" H., 2⅜" W. $15.00–25.00.

Plate 217 • Twin bullet-shaped metal lighter. Painted blue. Made by New Method. Circa early 1930's. 2¼" H., 1⅛" W. $20.00–35.00.

Plate 218 • Plastic strike-type match lighter. Head of the match comes off to light. Circa mid-1930's. 4" H., ½" Dia. $20.00–30.00.

Plate 219 • Television table lighter made by Swank. Circa early 1960's. 2¾" H., 3⅞" W. $30.00–50.00.

Plate 220 • Clear plastic and chromium Vu-Lighter with a tin box and instructions. Made by Scripto. Circa late 1950's. 2¾" H., 1½" W. $40.00–60.00.

Plate 221 • "Lucky Key" made of brass. Circa mid-1960's. 1¾" H., ⅜" W. $25.00–40.00.

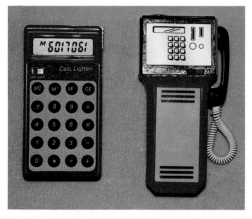

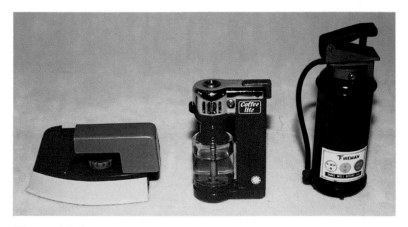

Plate 222 • Butane pocket lighters from Germany. Both circa 1990. (a) Calculator. 2½" H., 1¼" W. $10.00–20.00. (b) Pay phone. 2⅞" H., 1¼" W. $15.00–25.00.

Plate 223 • Butane pocket lighters from Germany. All circa 1990. (a) Iron. 1¼" H., 2⅜" W. $15.00–25.00. (b) Coffee maker. 2⅛" H., 1¼" W. $15.00–25.00. (c) Fire extinguisher. 3" H., 1" W. $15.00–25.00.

Plate 224 • Butane pocket lighters from Germany. All circa 1990. (a) Golf clubs and bag. 2⅞" H., 1⅜" W. $15.00–25.00. (b) Soccer field. 2¼" H., 1¼" W. $15.00–25.00. (c) Camera. 1½" H., 2¼" W. $15.00–25.00.

Plate 225 • Metal butane table lighter resembling a Yamaha generator. Has a digital clock. Circa early 1980's. 4½" H., 5¾" W. $30.00–45.00.

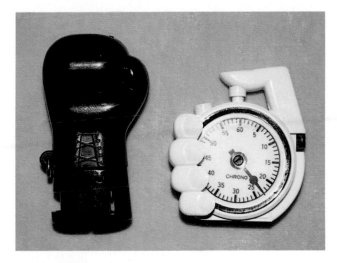

Plate 226 • Butane pocket lighters from Germany. Both circa 1990. (a) Boxing glove. 2⅝" H., 1⅜" W. $15.00–25.00. (b) Stop watch. 2⅛" H., 2" W. $15.00–25.00.

Plate 227 • Painted metal Model T Ford. (Lighter behind the seat.) Circa 1960. 1¼" H., 3⅛" W. $15.00–25.00.

Plate 228, 229 • Motel T Ford table lighter with cigarette holder. Made of plastic, painted metal, and rubber. To operate lighter, turn the spare tire. Roll the car forward to open the cigarette holder. (Right photo shows cigarette holder and lighter lid opened.) Circa 1950. 4" H., 6½" W. $50.00–70.00.

Plate 230 • Chromium motorcycle table lighter. (Front wheel turns right to left.) Uses butane fuel. Circa mid-1980's. 3½" H., 6" W. $35.00–50.00.

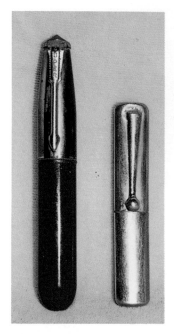

Plate 231 • Pocket clip-type lighters. Circa late 1940's. (a) Brass lighter is painted to look like an ink pen. Made by Super. 3¼" H., ½" Dia. $15.00–25.00. (b) Tin case. 2½" H., ½" W. $10.00–20.00.

Plate 232 • Two-toned plastic chair with a chromium lighter. Circa mid-1960's. 4" H., 2" W. $15.00–25.00.

Plate 233 • Painted chromium table or pocket lighter with box and instructions. Circa 1940's. 3" H., ¾" Dia. $30.00–45.00.

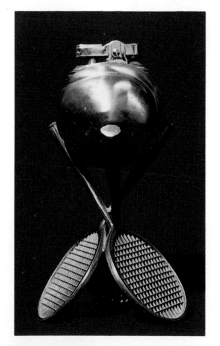

Plate 234 • Large chromium table lighter. Made in Japan. Circa late 1950's. 6½" H., 4½" W. $30.00–45.00.

Plate 235 • Chromium tennis ball with racquets for base. Circa mid-1960's. 6" H., 3¼" W. $20.00–30.00.

Plate 236 • Plastic ice cream cone table lighter. Circa early 1960's. 3⅝" H., 2½" W. $25.00–40.00.

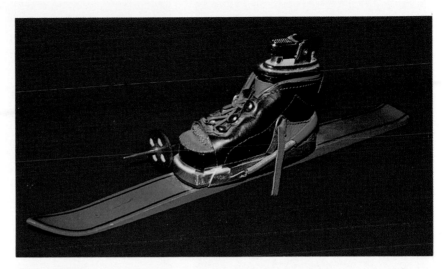

Plate 237 • Plastic eight-ball table lighter. Circa mid-1960's. 3" H., 2½" W. $15.00–25.00.

Plate 238 • Wooden ski, leather boot, and metal pole table lighter. Circa mid-1960's. 2¾" H., 9⅛" W. $15.00–25.00.

Plate 239 • "Retro-lite" plastic butane pocket lighters that look like old matchbook covers. Made by Scripto. Circa 1992. 2⅝" H., 1⅛" W. $5.00–10.00 each.

Plate 240 • Chromium table or pocket lighters shaped like bottles with paper labels. Made by KEM Inc., Liters. Circa 1948. 2⅝" H., ⅝" Dia. $20.00–30.00 each.

Plate 241 • Chromium camera pocket lighter. Made in Occupied Japan. Circa 1948. 1¾" H., 2½" W. $60.00–75.00.

Plate 242 • Metal, chromium, and leather camera on a tripod. Shutter release cable operates lighter. Made in Occupied Japan. Circa 1948. 3" H., 2½" W. $80.00–100.00.

Plate 243 • Camera table lighter on a tripod. Made in Occupied Japan. Circa 1948. 5" H., 2¾" W. $90.00–110.00.

Plate 244 • Pot-bellied stove lighter made of brass painted black. Circa mid-1950's. 5½" H., 2½" W. $15.00–30.00.

Plate 246 • Brass locomotive table lighter. (Roof is hinged to reveal the lighter.) Circa early 1960's. 2¼" H., 4¾" W. $20.00–40.00.

Plate 245 • Brass Model T Ford. (To operate lighter, press the horn on the left side of the hood.) Made in Japan. Circa mid-1950's. 3⅛" H., 5" W. $20.00–35.00.

Plate 247 • Brass tank table lighter. (To operate the lighter, push the button on the rear of tank.) Made in Japan. Circa early 1950's. 1¾" H., 5¾" W. $30.00–65.00.

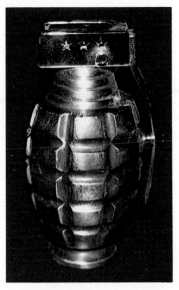

Plate 248 • Small Sarome "Blue Bird" table or pocket lighter. Made of painted chromium. Circa mid-1960's. 1⅛" H., 3⅛" W. $25.00–45.00.

Plate 249 • Chromium butane table lighter in the shape of a hand grenade. Made by P.G.L. Circa 1960. 4¼" H., 2½" W. $15.00–30.00.

Plate 250, 251 • Coin style pocket lighters. (Back view shown on right.) Circa mid-1960's. 1¼" Dia. $5.00–10.00 each.

Plate 252 • Ceramic beer stein table lighter from Germany. Circa 1958. 3¾" H., 1⅝" Dia. $45.00–60.00.

Plate 253 • Wooden barrel table lighter with a painted swan. Circa 1960's. 3¾" H., 2" Dia. $15.00–25.00.

Plate 254 • Painted metal barrel table lighter. Circa mid-1950's. 2½" H., 1⅝" Dia. $20.00–30.00.

Plate 255 • Brass stove lighter. (Chimney comes off to reveal lighter.) Circa mid-1950's. 3¼" H., ½" W. $10.00–20.00.

Plate 256 • Brass golf clubs and bag made by Negbaur. Circa 1939. 5" H., 1½" W. $75.00–100.00.

Plate 257 • Cowboy boot table lighter made by Evans. Circa 1948. 5" H., 5" W. $40.00–60.00.

Plate 258 • Barrette made by Stuart. (Perfume bottles converted to lighters.) Circa 1939. 4¾" H., 5" W. $45.00–60.00.

Plate 259 • Slot machine table lighter. Operates on batteries and butane. (When the arm is pulled, the images spin and the flame lights from above.) Circa mid-1960's. 6¾" H., 6" W. $30.00–45.00.

Plate 260 • Chromium and plastic engine table lighter. Touch tip style. Made by Remler Co. Ltd. Circa 1947. 3½" H., 5¼" W. $125.00–175.00.

Plate 261 • Hand-painted wooden shoe lighter. This is a souvenir of Holland. Circa 1940's. 2⅛" H., 4½" W. $20.00–40.00.

Plate 262 • Green plastic torpedo-shaped pocket lighter. Circa late 1930's. 3⅛" H., ⅝" Dia. $15.00–25.00.

— OCCUPIED JAPAN —

Plate 264 • Chromium car table lighter. (When the button on the left fender is pushed, the hood opens and the lighter is lit.) Made in Occupied Japan. Circa 1948. 1" H., 3" W. $80.00–110.00.

Plate 263 • Chromium bird cage table lighter. (The bird feeder at the bottom of the cage is the lighter.) Made in Occupied Japan. Circa early 1950's. 5½" H., 4" W. $200.00–250.00.

Plate 265 • Chromium rocket ship table lighter. (Squeeze the rear fins together to light.) Made in Occupied Japan. Circa 1949. 2" H., 5⅛" W. $80.00–110.00.

Plate 266, 267 • Chromium lift arm pocket lighter with mother-of-pearl inlay. Made in Occupied Japan. Circa 1948. (Right photo shows back view of lighter.) 2⅛" H., 1½" W. $80.00–110.00.

Plate 268 • Knight table lighters. All are made in Occupied Japan. Circa 1948. (a) 3½" H., 1½" W. (b) Made without a shield, but has a stand. 4" H., 1½" W. (c) 3½" H., 1½" W. $75.00–90.00 each.

Plate 269 • Chromium camera lighter with leather band and a tripod with telescoping legs. Shown with gift box. Made in Occupied Japan. Circa 1948. 3⅞" H., 2⅝" W. $100.00–125.00.

Plate 270 • Silverplated table lighter. Made in Occupied Japan. Circa 1948. 2¼" H., 2½" W. $60.00–80.00.

Plate 271 • "Patricia" silverplated over blue glass table lighter. Made in Occupied Japan. Circa 1949. 3¼" H., 4½" W. $90.00–110.00.

Plate 272 • Silverplated table lighter. Made in Occupied Japan. Circa 1948. 2¾" H., 3" W. $50.00–70.00.

Plate 273 • Chromium ship table lighter with red plastic detailing below lighter. Made in Occupied Japan. Circa 1950. 2" H., 5" W. $75.00–90.00.

Plate 274, 275 • Silverplated cowboy boot table lighters. Made in Occupied Japan. Circa 1950. (a) Has roses on the boot. 3" H., 3½" W. $50.00–70.00. (b) Has flowers on the side of the boot and stitching on the toe. 2¾" H., 2¾" W. $50.00–70.00.

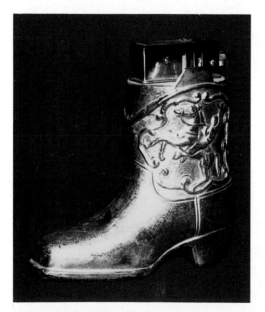  

Plate 276, 277 • Silverplated cowboy boot table lighters. Made in Occupied Japan. Circa 1950. (a) Has cowboy riding a horse on the side. (This boot was made without a spur.) 3¼" H., 3¼" W. $65.00–80.00. (b) Tall boot with a flowery vine on the side. 4¼" H., 3½" W. $50.00–75.00.

Plate 278 • Silverplated emperor table lighter. Made in Occupied Japan. Circa 1948. 3¼" H., 3½" W. $50.00–70.00.

Plate 279 • Chromium and plastic piano table lighter. (Push down on the keyboard to light.) Made in Occupied Japan. Circa 1948. 3¼" H., 2⅝" W. $115.00–130.00.

Plate 280 • Silverplated barrel table lighter. Made in Occupied Japan. Circa 1948. 3" H., 1¾" Dia. $60.00–80.00.

Plate 281 • Silverplated owl with glass eyes table lighter. Made in Occupied Japan. Circa 1948. 3" H., 2" W. $90.00–110.00.

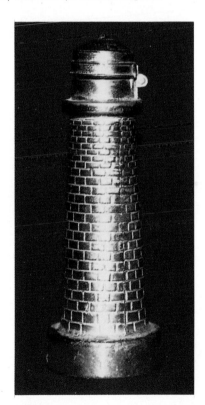

Plate 282 • Chromium telephone table lighter. (Take the receiver off and turn the dial to light.) Made in Occupied Japan. Circa 1948. 2¼" H., 3½" W. $100.00–130.00.

Plate 283 • Silverplated lighthouse table lighter. Made in Occupied Japan. Circa 1948. 4¼" H., 1½" Dia at base. $60.00–90.00.

Plate 284 • Brass pipe table lighter. Made in Occupied Japan. Circa 1948. 2¾" H., 4½" W. $50.00–70.00

Plate 285 • Metal gas pump table lighter. (Squeeze the nozzle to operate lighter.) Made in Occupied Japan. Circa 1949. 3½" H., 1¼" W. $75.00–100.00.

Plate 286 • Ceramic cat/lamp table lighter. Cat sitting next to lamp atop book. Lamp shade is hand-painted. (Pull chain under the shade to light.) Made in Occupied Japan. Circa 1948. 5¼" H., 2¾" W. $90.00–110.00.

— PRE-1940'S POCKET LIGHTERS —

Plate 287, 288 • Front and back views of brass pocket lighters. (The wick cap has to be unscrewed and taken off to light.) Circa 1918. (a) 3⅛" H., 2⅜" W. $100.00–150.00. (b) 3" H., 2⅜" W. $100.00–150.00.

Plate 289 • Brass pocket lighters shaped like books. Both circa 1918. Both are 2½" H., 1¾" W. $100.00–150.00 each.

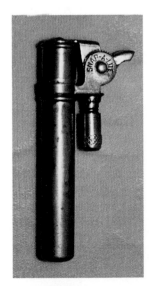   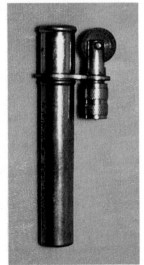

Plate 290 • Brass pocket lighter made by Snap-A-Lite. Circa 1913. 2½" H., 1" W. $40.00–60.00.

Plate 291 • Chromium pocket lighter. (Remove cap to operate lighter.) Circa 1922. 2⅛" H., 1¼" W. $30.00–50.00.

Plate 292 • Chromium pocket lighter made in Austria. Circa 1925. 2½" H., 1¼" W. $35.00–55.00.

Plate 293 • Chromium pocket lighter by Novitas Sales Co. Circa 1920. 2⅝" H., 1" W. $50.00–70.00.

Plate 294, 295 • Round brass pocket lighters. Circa 1918. Shown are front and back views of each. (a) Has unique slide cap over the wick. 2½" H., 1¾" W. $125.00–150.00. (b) 2½" H., 1¾" W. $100.00–150.00.

Plate 296 • Black plastic and chromium pocket lighter made by LECTRoLITE. Circa 1930's. 2" H., 1½" W. $30.00–40.00.

Plate 297 • Chromium lift arm pocket lighter with leather band made by Superfine. Circa late 1920's. 1⅞" H., 1½" W. 70.00–90.00.

Plate 298 • Brass and enamel pocket lighter with a unique windscreen. (It was sometimes used as a table lighter because of its size and beauty.) Made by Evans. Circa 1934. 2⅜" H., 2¼" W. $40.00–50.00.

Plate 299 • Brass pocket lighter with unique slide cap over the wick. Made by Parker in Austria. "U.S. Pat. Apr. 2, 1912." Circa 1913. 2⅜" H., 1¼" W. $70.00–90.00.

Plate 300 • Brass and Bakelite lift arm pocket lighter. Made by MAY FAIR. Circa mid-1930's. 2" H., 1⅝" W. $70.00–90.00.

Plate 301 • Sterling silver lift arm pocket lighter made in Mexico. Circa late 1930's. 1⅝" H., 1⅝" W. $30.00–55.00.

Plate 302 • Chromium pocket lighter made by Perfecto. Circa 1930. 2½" H., 1½" W. $40.00–55.00.

Plate 303 • Chromium pocket lighter made by Thorens. Circa early 1930's. 2⅜" H., 1½" W. $50.00–65.00.

Plate 304 • Chromium pocket lighter made by Regens. Circa 1933. 2⅛" H., 1¼" W. $20.00–40.00.

Plate 305 • Chromium pocket lighter with lift-off wick cap. Made by Derby. "Patented April 2, 1912." Circa 1913. 2½" H., ⅞" W. $50.00–70.00.

Plate 306 • Chromium pocket lighters made by MYFLAM in England. All circa 1937. (a) 1¾" H., 1⅝" W. $50.00–75.00. (b) Floral design. 1½" H., 1⅜" W. $40.00–60.00. (c) Leather band. 1½" H., 1⅜" W. $40.00–60.00.

Plate 307, 308 • Round brass pocket lighters. (Front and back designs shown.) Both are circa 1918. (a) Wick cap unscrews. 2⅜" H., 1⅝" W. $100.00–150.00. (b) Has a unique lift arm. 2¼" H., 1⅝" W. $150.00–175.00.

Plate 309 • Chromium lift arm pocket lighter. Checkerboard design on the cover. Circa mid-1930's. 1¾" H., 1½" W. $40.00–60.00.

Plate 310 • Chromium pocket lighter with built-in windscreen. Circa 1932. 2⅛" H., 1½" W. $40.00–60.00.

Plate 311 • Silverplated pocket lighter by Evans. Circa 1934. 2" H., 1½" W. $20.00–40.00.

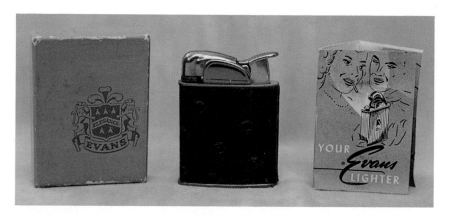

Plate 312 • Brass pocket lighter with ostrich hide band. Shown with gift box and instructions. Made by Evans. Circa 1934. 2" H., 1½" W. $50.00–70.00.

Plate 313, 314 • Round brass pocket lighters. (Front and back designs shown.) Both are circa 1918. (a) 2½" H., 1¾" W. $100.00–150.00. (b) 2⅜" H., 1¾" W. $100.00–150.00.

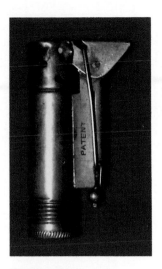 

Plate 315 • Chromium lift arm pocket lighter by TEE-VEE. Circa mid-1930's. 1½" H., ⅞" W. $15.00–25.00.

Plate 316 • Chromium pocket lighter with adjustable windscreen cover. Made by IMCO. Circa 1935. 2½" H., 1¼" W. $10.00–25.00.

Plate 317 • Brass pocket lighter made in Austria. Circa 1925. 2⅜" H., 1½" W. $35.00–50.00.

Plate 318 • Silver lift arm pocket lighter made by Colibri. Circa 1937. 2½" H., 1⅜" W. $110.00–140.00.

Plate 319 • Chromium pocket lighter with a leather band. It has a unique lighter mechanism. Made by CHAMP-O-MATIC in Austria. Circa mid-1930's. 1¾" H., 1½" W. $25.00–45.00.

Plate 320 • Brass pocket lighter. Circa 1918. 1¼" H., 1⅝" W. $60.00–80.00.

Plate 321 • "Standard" chromium pocket lighter by Ronson. Circa 1935. 2" H., 1⅝" W. $50.00–70.00.

Plate 322, 323 • Chromium and leather pocket lighter that had to be hand wound to operate. (Front and back shown.) Made by Henry Automatic. Circa mid-1920's. 2½" H., 1¾" W. $80.00–110.00.

Plate 324 • Chromium pocket lighter. Small flat center opens to light –a unique operation. Made by Colby. Circa 1935. 2⅜" H., 1⅛" W. $90.00–110.00.

Plate 325 • Chromium pocket lighter made by Speed. Circa 1938. 2⅛" H., 1⅞" W. $75.00–90.00.

Plate 326 • Chromium pocket lighter made by Zenith. Circa 1938. 2½" H., 1½" W. $15.00–30.00.

Plate 327 • Chromium pocket lighter made by Thorens. "Pat. Nov. 16, 1920." Circa 1921. 1⅞" H., 1⅛" W. $50.00–75.00.

Plate 328 • Brass cylinder lighter made by Redilite. Circa 1928. 2⅞" H., ⅜" Dia. $10.00–20.00.

Plate 329 • Chromium pocket lighter with red leather insert band. Made by Evans. Circa 1934. 2" H., 1½" W. $25.00–40.00.

Plate 330 • Brass and silverplated pocket lighter with basket weave design. Made by Evans. Circa 1934. 1½" H., 1½" W. $40.00–60.00.

Plate 331 • Chromium lift arm pocket lighter with leather band. Made by Napier in France. Circa late 1930's. 1⅞" H., 1¾" W. $80.00–100.00.

Plate 332 • Chromium and enamel pocket lighter. (By pressing the stem inward, the center slides open to light.) Made by D.P.R. in Germany. Circa 1929. 1¾" H., 2¼" W. $110.00–140.00.

Plate 335 • Chromium lift arm pocket lighter with leather band and plate for engraving initials. Made by Golden Wheel. Circa 1928. 1¾" H., 1⅝" W. $60.00–80.00.

Plate 333 • Chromium lift arm pocket lighter made by Camel. Circa mid-1930's. 2¼" H., 1¼" W. $25.00–40.00.

Plate 334 • Chromium pocket lighter made by IMACO. Circa 1938. 2¼" H., 1⅛" W. $10.00–25.00.

Plate 336 • Brass pocket lighter with a leather band made by Evans. Circa 1934. 1½" H., 1½" W. $30.00–45.00.

Plate 337 • Tin-painted pocket lighter. Circa 1930's. 1⅞" H., ¾" W. $10.00–25.00.

Plate 338 • Goldplated pocket lighter made by Evans. Circa 1934. 2" H., 1½" W. $40.00–60.00.

Plate 339 • Sterling silver pocket lighter made by D.P.R. in Germany. Circa early 1930's. 1⅞" H., 1½" W. $90.00–110.00.

Plate 340• Chromium and leather lift arm pocket lighter with built-in watch made by Triangle. Circa 1928. 1¾" H., 1¾" W. $250.00–300.00.

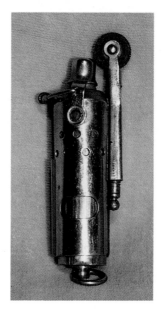

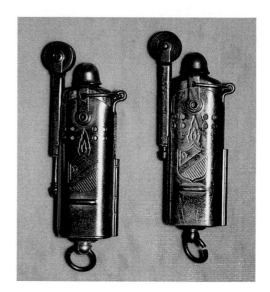

Plate 341 • Tin case with brass lighter. Circa late 1930's. 3" H., 1⅛" W. $20.00–40.00.

Plate 342 • Chromium trench-style pocket lighter made in Austria. Circa 1918. 3" H., 1" W. $30.00–50.00.

Plate 343 • Trench-style pocket lighters. Both circa 1918. One is made of chromium; the other is brass. Both measure 2⅞" H., 1" W. $30.00–50.00 each.

Plate 344 • Chromium and tortoise enamel lift arm pocket lighter. Shown with gift box. Circa late 1920's. 1⅞" H., 1½" W. $90.00–110.00.

Plate 345 • Chromium and leather pocket lighter. (Has eye viewer in the center that has risque photos.) Made in Japan by Globe. Circa mid-1930's. $100.00–125.00.

Plate 346 • Chromium and leather lift arm pocket made by Triangle. Circa late 1920's. 1⅞" H., 1½" W. $60.00–80.00.

Plate 347 • Chromium lift arm pocket lighters. (a) Circa mid-1920's. 1¾" H., 1⅜" W. $25.00–40.00. (b) Circa late 1920's. 1⅝" H., 1½" W. $25.00–40.00.

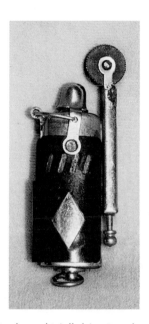

Plate 348 • Chromium lift arm pocket lighter made by Evans. Circa late 1920's. 2⅛" H., 1½" W. $35.00–50.00.

Plate 349 • Early "Duplex" pocket lighter in chromium and enamel. (Leather band missing.) Made by Ronson. Circa 1929. 2½" H., 1½" W. $80.00–110.00.

Plate 350 • Brass and steel pocket lighter made in Germany by D.P.R. Circa 1922. 2½" H., ⅞" W. $50.00–75.00.

Plate 351 • Chromium and painted enamel lighter made in Japan. Circa 1920's. 2½" H., ⅞" W. $20.00–35.00.

Plate 352 • Chromium pocket or table lighter made by Evans. Circa 1934. 2" H., 1⅞" W. $25.00–35.00.

Plate 353 • Chromium and leather lift arm pocket lighter with a built-in windscreen. Made by Golden Wheel. Circa late 1920's. 2⅛" H., 1¾" W. $60.00–80.00.

Plate 354 • Silver lift arm pocket lighter with leather band and windscreen. Made by Dunhill. Circa 1912. 2⅛" H., 1¾" W. $275.00–325.00.

Plate 355 • "Gem" chromium lift arm pocket lighters with leather band. Made by Rex Mfg. Co. Circa 1930's. 2" H., 1⅜" W. $30.00–50.00 each.

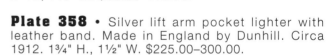

Plate 356 • Goldplated lift arm pocket lighter with gift box made by Clark. Circa late 1930's. 2⅛" H., 1½" W. $80.00–100.00.

Plate 357 • A unique lift arm pocket lighter made in chromium and leather by Marathon. Circa 1925. 2" H., 1½" W. $80.00–110.00.

Plate 358 • Silver lift arm pocket lighter with leather band. Made in England by Dunhill. Circa 1912. 1¾" H., 1½" W. $225.00–300.00.

Plate 359 • 18-karat gold electroplated lift arm pocket lighter with leather band. Made by Clark. "Pat. July 27, 1926." Circa 1927. 1⅞" H., 1½" W. $60.00–85.00.

Plate 360 • Chromium pocket lighter. Circa 1935. 1⅞" H., 1½" W. $10.00–25.00.

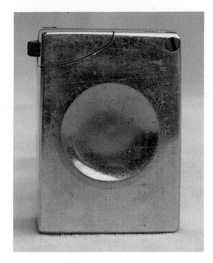

Plate 361 • Chromium pocket lighter. Made in Germany by R.K. Modell. Circa 1912. 2⅛" H., 1¼" W. $70.00–90.00.

Plate 362 • Chromium lift arm pocket lighter made by AERO-LITE. Circa mid-1930's. 2⅛" H., 1" W. $20.00–30.00.

Plate 363 • Chromium lift arm pocket lighter made by TEE-VEE. Circa mid-1930's. 1¾" H., 1¼" W. $20.00–35.00.

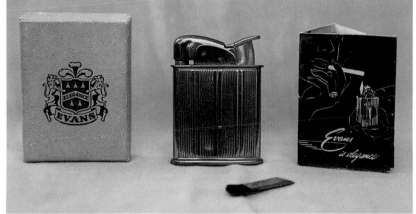

Plate 364 • Goldplated pocket lighter with gift box, instructions, and cleaning brush. Made by Evans. Circa 1934. 2" H., 1½" W. $75.00–90.00.

Plate 365 • Chromium and brass lift arm pocket lighter. Circa late 1920's. 2⅛" H., 1½" W. $35.00–50.00.

Plate 366 • Chromium pocket lighter made by Evans. Circa 1929. 2" H., 1½" W. $50.00–70.00.

Plate 367 • Early chromium pocket lighter made by Thorens. Circa mid-1930's. 2⅛" H., 1½" W. $40.00–60.00.

Plate 368 • Chromium pocket lighter by Thorens. Circa early 1930's. 2⅛" H., 1½" W. $50.00–70.00.

Plate 369 • Chromium pocket lighter with leather band. Circa 1930's. 1¾" H., 1½" W. $50.00–70.00.

Plate 370 • Chromium and leather pocket lighter that has a different type of lighting mechanism. Made by Morton. Circa mid-1930's. 2" H., 1⅝" W. $80.00–100.00.

Plate 371 • Chromium and leather lift arm pocket lighter made by Superfine. Circa early 1930's. 1⅞" H., 1½" W. $70.00–90.00

Plate 372 • Goldplated lift arm pocket lighter made by Rexlite. Circa late 1920's. 1¾" H., 1½" W. $75.00–100.00.

Plate 373, 374 • Chromium lift arm pocket lighters. (a) Made by Sharpo. Circa 1935. 2⅜" H., ⅞" W. $35.00–50.00. (b) Made by Cygnus. Circa 1928. 2½" H., 1" W. $25.00–40.00.

Plate 375 • "Gem" brass lift arm pocket lighter made by Rex Mfg. Co. Circa 1930's. 2" H., 1⅜" W. $30.00–50.00.

Plate 376, 377 • Brass and Bakelite pocket lighter with a unique lift arm. Commemorates the 10th Olympiad. Circa 1932. (Front and back is shown.) 2¼" H., 1¾" W. $80.00–100.00.

Plate 378 • Chromium pocket lighter made in Austria. Circa 1918. 2¼" H., 1⅜" W. $75.00–100.00.

Plate 379 • (a) Brass pocket lighter with German wording that translates to *God Is With Us.* Circa 1918. 2⅝" H., 2" W. $100.00–150.00. (b) Small brass pocket lighter. Circa 1918. 2" H., 1½" W. $50.00–75.00.

Plate 380 • Early chromium "Magic Pocket Lamp and Cigar Lighter" with gift box and tin for the flint disk. "Koopmans Pat. Oct. 29, 89" [sole mfrs] New York. Circa 1890. 2½" H., 1¾" W. $225.00–275.00.

On next page are the instructions for the "Magic Pocket Lamp."

DIRECTIONS.

ALSO A FEW SUGGESTIONS TO THE USER OF THE
MAGIC POCKET LAMP.

No. 2.

No. 1.

No. 3.

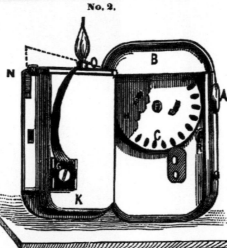

SHOWING LAMP OPEN AND BEING LIGHTED.

SHOWING METHOD OF FILLING LAMP.

This article is neither a Toy nor a Humbug, but a Practical Mechanical Device, which, with a proper treatment at your hands, and by following the directions given below, will prove most convenient, and amply repay you for any little attention you may bestow upon it.

TO LIGHT: Press the Button (A) until it comes to a stop; this opens cover (B) and lights lamp also. If no light is desired, merely press Button (A), until cover flies open; a pressure of Button to a stop will light the lamp as well after cover is open. It will thus be seen that opening cover and lighting lamp can be done separately or together, without interference or injury to the lighter.

To Open for Renewing Lights,&c. First open Cover (B). Then press down Spring Catch (N); this releases Latch Hook (R) and opens door. *Never try to force door (K) open, or close same, when cover (B) is closed.*

TO RENEW LIGHTING DISK: Place Cardboard Disk (C) upon Rotary Carrier (H) so that the round hole in disk fits over center-pin (F) of carrier; rest the thumb with slight pressure on face of disk, and gently turn it from left to right until the fasteners (D,D) have entered the two slits in disk, when half a turn further locks disk to carrier.

TO REMOVE DISK: Turn the disk from right to left until released from fasteners (D,D), when it can be lifted off center-pin F.) Reverse the disk, and you have a fresh supply of lights on the other side.

TO CHARGE LAMP WITH FLUID: With ordinary usage one filling per week should be sufficient. *The Oil Box (K) must not be filled* with oil. It is intended that the *cotton packing should be only saturated.* A simple test as to correct quantity is to invert the box before closing its lid, and see that no fluid escapes, thus avoiding any possible soiling of the clothing when in use. See Cut No. 3 above for method of filling.

FLUID. When our specially prepared fluid (furnished with Lamp) cannot be procured, we recommend the use of Highest Grade Refined Head Light Oil.

WICK: The wick will last a considerable time, and can be drawn up as required. The brass tip at one end of same is to allow the wick to be easily inserted.

Cut No. 2 shows the proper position of lamp when a portable or stationary light of more than a moment's duration is required.

Keep Your Lamp Clean.   This is Important.

An occasional cleaning of any deposit which may collect around wick occupies but a few moments, and will insure a satisfactory working of the lamp.

All parts of the lamp are interchangeable, and should they become worn out, can be replaced at a trifling cost by communicating with us.

We are anxious that the Magic Pocket Lamp should prove a useful and satisfactory article to you, and we will contribute all in our power to make it so.

MAGIC POCKET LAMP OUTFIT.

Consisting of neat, leather covered case. containing..................................... { 1 Magic Pocket Lamp.
1 Bottle Special Magic Oil.
1000 Extra Lights.
1 Feeder for properly filling Lamp.

RETAIL PRICE..each, $1.00.

BOX OF 1000 EXTRA LIGHTS.

As our goods are not mailable under the U. S. Postal Laws, they must invariably be sent by Express or Freight.
RETAIL PRICE...............per box, 10c.

— POST-1940'S POCKET LIGHTERS —

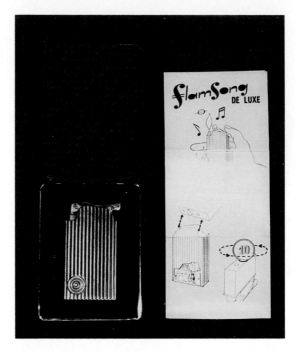

Plate 381 • "Flaminaire" chromium butane pocket lighter with gift box made by Parker. Circa 1951. 2¾" H., 1⅜" W. $30.00–50.00.

Plate 382 • Musical pocket lighter in gift box and instructions. Plays "Two Cigarettes In The Dark." Made in Switzerland by Reuge. Circa late 1940's. 2⅝" H., 1⅜" W. $90.00–110.00.

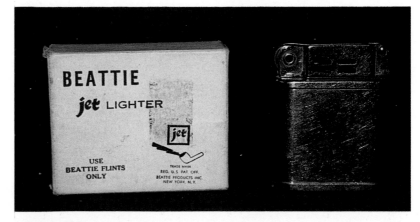

Plate 383 • Chromium lift arm pocket lighter made in England. Circa 1948. 1¾" H., 1¼" W. $80.00–100.00.

Plate 384 • Chromium pocket pipe lighter with gift box made by Beattie. Circa early 1950's. 2⅛" H., 1¾" W. $30.00–50.00.

Plate 385 • Pocket lighters made by Colibri. Circa 1955. (a) Goldplated lighter. (b) Chromium lighter with tortoise enamel. (c) Chromium lighter. All measure 1½" H., 1⅝" W. $30.00–50.00 each.

 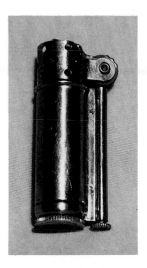  

Plate 386 • Chromium pocket lighter made by Evans. Circa late 1940's. 2" H., 1½" W. $25.00–45.00.

Plate 387 • Chromium service lighter made in England by Dunhill. Circa early 1940's. 2⁵⁄₁₆" H., 1⅛" W. $35.00–50.00.

Plate 388 • Brass replica lift arm pocket lighter. Circa 1985. 2¼" H., ¾" W. $15.00–30.00.

Plate 389 • Chromium musical pocket lighter made by Prince. Circa 1960's. 2⅛" H., 1¾" W. $30.00–50.00.

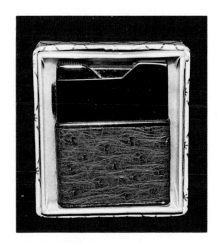 

Plate 391 • Chromium pocket lighter with gift box. Circa late 1940's. 2⅛" H., 1¾" W. $30.00–45.00.

Plate 390 • Brass lighter with leather band made by Elgin American. Shown in gift box. Circa early 1960's. 1¾" H., 1⅜" W. $40.00–60.00.

Plate 392 • "Adonis" blue enamel pocket lighter with ivory cherubs. Shown with gift box. Made by Ronson. Circa 1954. 1¾" H., 2⅛" W. $40.00–60.00.

Plate 393 • "Capri" blue enamel pocket lighter with ivory cherubs. Shown with gift box made by Ronson. Circa 1954. 2⅛" H., 1¾" W. $45.00–75.00.

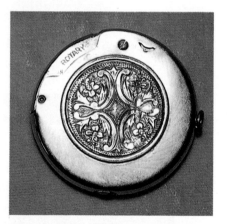

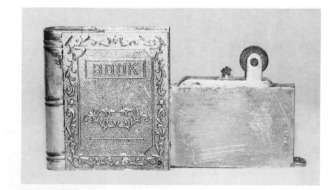

Plate 394 • Chromium heart-shaped pocket lighter. (Plastic insert colored to simulate mother-of-pearl.) Made by Continental. Circa mid-1950's. 2" H., 2" W. $15.00–25.00.

Plate 395 • Round chromium pocket lighter made by Prince. Circa late 1950's. 1⅞" Dia. $20.00–30.00.

Plate 396 • Round chromium pocket lighter with a leather band made by Penguin. Circa late 1950's. 2" Dia. $30.00–40.00.

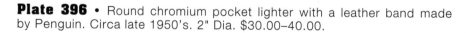

Plate 397 • Pouch style pocket lighter made by Colibri. Circa 1954. 2⅛" H., 2" W. $40.00–60.00.

Plate 398 • Chromium flip-out type book lighter. Circa late 1950's. 1½" H., 1¼" W. $20.00–30.00.

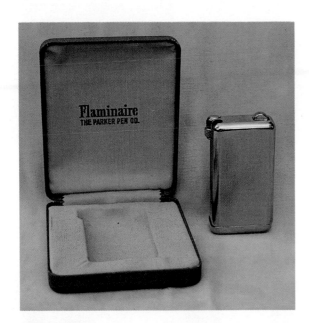

Plate 399 • Chromium butane pocket lighter with a gift box made by Parker. Circa 1951. (Similar to Plate 381.) 2¾" H., 1⅜" W. $30.00–50.00.

Plate 400 • Chromium tube-style pocket lighter. Circa late 1950's. 2⅜" H., ⅜" Dia. $5.00–15.00.

Plate 401 • Goldplated lift arm pocket lighter made by Dunhill. Circa 1950's. 3" H., ⅞" W. $225.00–275.00.

Plate 402 • Chromium double wick lighter made by DUB-L-LITE. Circa 1948. 2¼" H., 1½" W. $40.00–50.00.

Plate 403 • Chromium lift arm pocket lighter with a leather band. Made by Continental. Circa late 1940's. 2⅛" H., 1½" W. $65.00–90.00.

Plate 404 • Chromium and brass finish lighter made by Elgin American. Circa late 1940's. 1¾" H., 2⅛" W. $25.00–40.00.

Plate 405 • "Adonis" pocket lighters made by Ronson. Circa 1947. Both measure 1⅞" H., 2⅛" W. (a) Chromium and black enamel. $25.00–40.00. (b) Silverplated. $40.00–50.00.

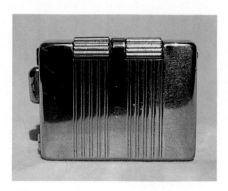

Plate 406 • Brass with ivory colored band made by Pigeon. Circa early 1960's. 1⅜" H., 1¾" W. $20.00–30.00.

Plate 407 • Chromium butane pocket lighter made by Strato Flame. Circa 1952. 1¾" H., 2¼" W. $25.00–40.00.

Plate 408 • Chromium and leather pocket lighter made by Continental. Circa mid-1950's. 1¼" H., 1¼" W. $10.00–20.00.

Plate 409 • Goldplated musical pocket lighter with gift box. Plays "Home On The Range." Made by CROWN. Circa late 1940's. 2⅝" H., 1¾" W. $60.00–80.00.

Plate 410 • Chromium pocket lighter with changeable calendar. Circa early 1960's. 2¼" H., 1½" W. $30.00–40.00.

Plate 411 • Chromium pocket lighter with leather band. Has fuel view finder Made by Hilton. Circa mid-1950's. 2" H., 1⅝" W. $10.00–20.00.

Plate 412 • Chromium pocket lighter with plastic leather-like band made in Austria by Champ. Circa 1950's. 2¼" H., 1½" W. $10.00–20.00.

Plate 413 • Brass lift arm replica pocket lighter. Circa 1985. 1⅞" H., 1⅛" W. $15.00–25.00.

Plate 414 • Chromium butane Royale "2500" pocket lighter with view finder. Has gift box and instructions. Circa late 1950's. 1⅛" H., 2⅝" W. $30.00–40.00.

Plate 416 • Chromium and enamel pocket lighters with gift boxes. Made by Continental. Circa mid-1950's. 2" H., 1¼" W. $20.00–30.00 each.

Plate 415 • Silverplated butane lift arm pocket lighter with gift box. Made in England by Dunhill. Circa 1990. 2½" H., 1⅛" W. $225.00–250.00.

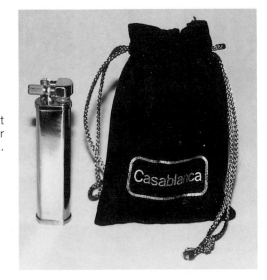

Plate 417 • "Casablanca" brass replica pocket lighter with a velvet draw string pouch. (The lighter has a secret compartment for money.) Circa 1985. 3¼" H., ¾" W. $20.00–30.00.

Plate 418 • Chromium and brass pocket lighter with enamel painted map of Texas on it. Made by Continental. Circa mid-1950's. 2" H., 1⅝" W. $40.00–50.00.

Plate 419 • "Essex" chromium and leather pocket lighter made by Ronson. Circa 1954. 2⅛" H., 1⅞" W. $20.00–30.00.

Plate 420 • Brass lighter with leather band made in Japan. Circa mid-1950's. 1½" H., 2⅛" W. $10.00–20.00.

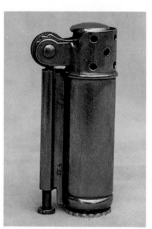

Plate 421 • Box of twelve chromium and black enamel service lighters made by Dunhill. Circa early 1940's. 2⅜" H., 1" W. $40.00–50.00 each.

Plate 422 • Chromium pocket service lighter made by Parker. Circa early 1940's. 2⁵⁄₁₆" H., 1¹⁄₁₆" W. $35.00–50.00.

Plate 423 • Chromium pocket lighter made by Regens. Circa 1948. 2⅛" H., 1¼" W. $15.00–25.00.

Plate 424 • Chromium pocket lighters made by Ronson. (a) "Standard." Circa early 1950's. 2" H., 1¾" W. $15.00–25.00. (b) "Whirlwind." Circa 1941. 2⅛" H., 1¾" W. $25.00–40.00. (c) "Princess." Circa early 1950's. 2" H., 1½" W. $15.00–25.00.

Plate 425 • "Typhoon" chromium with gift box and instructions made by Ronson. Circa 1960. (Bottom half in brush finish.) 2¼" H., 1½" W. $30.00–40.00.

Plate 426 • "Varaflame" chromium butane pocket lighter with gift box made in France by Ronson. Circa 1964. 1½" H., 2½" W. $30.00–50.00.

Plate 427 • Chromium lift arm replica pocket lighter with gift box made by Colibri. Circa 1986. 2⅝" H., 1¼" W. $65.00–80.00.

Plate 429 • Chromium pocket lighters made by Ronson. (a) "Standard." Circa early 1950's. 2⅛" H., 1½" W. $15.00–25.00. (b) "Whirlwind." Circa 1941. 2⅛" H., 1¾" W. $35.00–50.00.

Plate 428 • "Varaflame" chromium butane pocket lighter with gift box made by Ronson. Circa 1960's. 2¾" H., 1" W. $30.00–40.00.

Plate 430 • Chromium pocket lighter with box and instructions made by Nimrod. Circa early 1970's. 3⅛" H., ¾" W. $25.00–40.00.

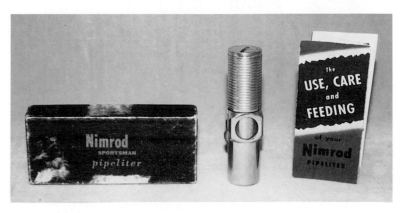

Plate 431 • Brass cylinder lighter painted blue and black. Made by BALLoFLINT. Circa late 1940's. 2⅝" H., ½" Dia. $20.00–30.00.

Plate 432 • Brass cylinder type pocket lighter. Made by ALL-BRIGHT. Circa early 1950's. 2½" H., ⅝" W. $20.00–30.00.

Plate 433 • Chromium and leather pocket lighter. Made by Royal Star. Circa 1954. 1⅝" H., 1⅜" W. $10.00–20.00.

Plate 434 • Brass musical pocket lighter. Plays "On The Atchison, Topeka, and The Santa Fe." Made by CROWN. Circa late 1940's. 2⅝" H., 1⅜" W. $75.00–90.00.

Plate 435 • Chromium and paint cylinder pocket lights. All are circa late 1940's. (a, b, d) 1½" H., ½" Dia. (c) 2" H., ½" Dia. $10.00–20.00 each.

— SETS —

Plate 436 • Brass and plastic table lighter with stand and four ashtrays. Made by A.S.R. Circa late 1940's. Lighter, 2¾" H., 1⅞" W. Ashtrays, 3" Dia. $45.00–60.00.

Plate 437 • Three-piece silverplated set. Made in Occupied Japan. Circa 1948. Lighter, 3" H., 2¾" Dia. Cigarette holder, 2¾" H., 2¾" Dia. Tray, 4" x 7¼". $80.00–100.00.

Plate 438 • Three-piece ceramic set with gold trim made by Evans. Circa late 1930's. Lighter, 2" H., 3" Dia. Cigarette holder, 2" H., 3" Dia. Ashtray, 1" H., 3" Dia. $50.00–60.00.

Plate 439 • Two-piece brass and ceramic set with gold trim made by Evans. Circa late 1930's. Lighter, 3" H., 3¾" W. Cigarette holder, 2⅜" H., 3¾" W. $70.00–90.00.

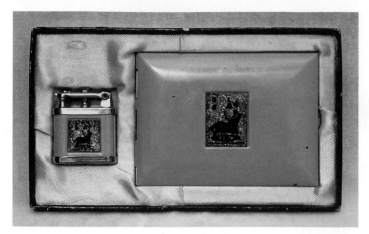

Plate 440 • Chromium and enamel lift arm lighter with cigarette case. Shown in gift box. Made by Girey. Circa 1935. Lighter, 1¾" H., 1½" W. Cigarette case, 3⅛" H., 4¼" W. $80.00–100.00.

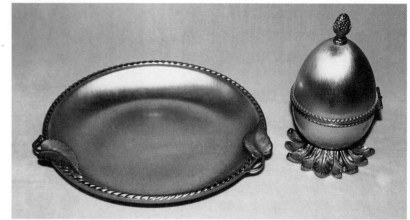

Plate 441 • Two-piece chromium set with brush finish and gold trim. Made by Evans. Circa mid-1950's. Lighter, 4½" H., 2¼" Dia. Ashtray, 1" H., 6" Dia. $50.00–75.00.

Plate 442 • Brass and leather covered cigarette case with lighter made by Evans. Circa mid-1930's. 1½" H., 6¼" W. $40.00–60.00.

Plate 443 • Four-piece metal set with lighter, ashtray, cigarette case, and tray made in Japan. Circa late 1930's. Overall size 2⅜" H., 10¼" W. $35.00–60.00.

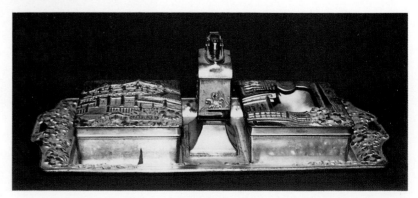

Plate 444 • Metal lighter, ashtray, and cigarette holder with built-in music box. Made in Japan. Circa late 1930's. 3" H., 9" W. $30.00–60.00.

Plate 445 • Two-piece ceramic set made of Delft glass. Circa 1930's. Each piece measures 1½" H., 3¼" W. $40.00–70.00.

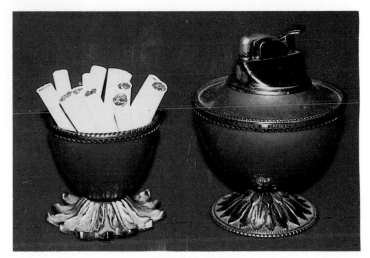

Plate 446 • Two-piece brass and enamel set made by Evans. Circa late 1950's. Lighter, 4" H., 3" Dia. Cigarette holder, 2¼" H., 2¼" Dia. $50.00–75.00.

Plate 447 • Two-piece chromium set made in Occupied Japan. Circa 1949. Lighter, 3" H., 4" W. Ashtray, 3¼" x 5½". $75.00–90.00.

— TABLE LIGHTERS —

Plate 448 • Chromium butane table lighter. Made in England by Ronson. Circa 1962. 4" H., 1¼" W. $20.00–30.00.

Plate 449 • "Moderne" chromium table lighter made by Zippo. Circa 1966. 4⅛" H., 2¼" Dia. at base. $35.00–50.00.

Plate 450 • Goldplated lift arm table lighter. (When lighter is set down, the arm comes down over the wick to snuff out the flame.) Made by Segal. Circa late 1920's. 4" H., 1½" W. $90.00–120.00.

Plate 451 • "Crown" quadruple silverplated table lighter made by Ronson. Circa 1936. 2¼" H., 2¾" W. $45.00–60.00.

Plate 452 • Chromium and ceramic table lighter. Circa 1960's. 2⅛" H., 1¾" W. $10.00–15.00.

Plate 453 • Chromium table lighter. Circa early 1960's. 2⅜" H., 1½" Dia at base. $15.00–25.00.

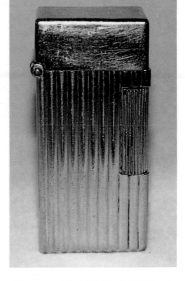

Plate 454 • Large chromium lift arm table lighter. Made in Occupied Japan. Circa 1950. 3⅞" H., 2⅞" W. $50.00–70.00.

Plate 455 • Brass table lighter. Circa mid-1920's. 2¾" H., 2⅛" W. $15.00–30.00.

Plate 456 • Chromium table lighter made by Parker. Circa mid-1930's. 3" H., 1⅜" W. $35.00–50.00.

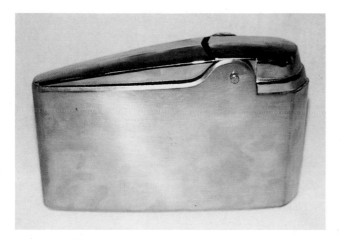

Plate 457 • Large chromium table lighter made by Shields. Circa late 1950's. 4½" H., 6⅝" W. $20.00–30.00.

Plate 458 • Chromium lift arm table lighter with mother-of-pearl inlays. Made in Occupied Japan. Circa 1948. 2⅛" H., 2" W. at base. $80.00–100.00.

Plate 459 • Painted brass replica lift arm table lighter. Uses butane fuel. Circa 1988. 3⅛" H., 2⅜" W. $15.00–25.00.

Plate 460 • "Georgian" silverplated table lighter made by Ronson. Circa 1936. 2½" H., 3¼" W. $45.00–60.00.

Plate 461 • Brass and leather table lighter. (Made to look like a bucket.) Made by Evans. Circa mid-1930's. 4¼" H., 2¼" W. $50.00–70.00.

Plate 462 • Chromium table lighter with painted base. Made by IMCO. Circa 1930. 2½" H., 2" W. at base. $20.00–30.00.

Plate 463 • Chromium and enamel table lighter with a unique windscreen. Made by Evans. Circa 1934. 2⅜" H., 2¼" W. $25.00–45.00.

Plate 465 • Fur covered brass table lighter. Made by Evans. Circa 1934. 3" H., 1¾" Dia. $35.00–50.00.

Plate 466 • Chromium table lighter. Made in England by Eclair. Circa mid-1930's. 4¼" H., 1½" Dia. at base. $100.00–120.00.

Plate 464 • Brass table lighter with a leather base. (Has a unique thumb slide mechanism on the side.) Made by Evans. Circa mid-1930's. 2⅛" H., 2½" Dia. $60.00–75.00.

Plate 467 • Chromium table lighter with leather band made by The Giant. 4" H., 3⅜" W. Circa early 1950's. $25.00–35.00.

Plate 469 • Chromium airplane table lighter. (Lights by turning the propeller.) Circa 1935. 3⅛" H., 5¾" W, 7¼" wing span. $110.00–140.00.

Plate 470 • Painted chromium airplane table lighter. (Lights by turning the propeller.) Circa 1935. 3" H., 6" W, 5" wing span. $80.00–100.00.

Plate 468 • Stainless steel table lighter shaped like a cognac glass. Circa 1960's. 5" H., 2¾" Dia. $15.00–25.00.

Plate 471 • Painted chromium airplane table lighter. (Lights by turning the propeller.) Very similar to lighter at top of page. Circa 1935. 3" H., 6" W, 5" wing span. $100.00–120.00.

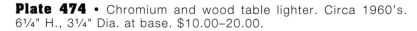

Plate 472 • Chromium tankard table lighter. Uses butane fuel. Circa early 1980's. 4¼" H., 3" W. $20.00–30.00.

Plate 473 • Brass table lighter. (Note the many levers and springs that operate this lighter.) Made by Capitol. "Patented Sept. 17, 1912." Circa 1913. 5" H., 2⅞" Dia. at base. $175.00–250.00.

Plate 474 • Chromium and wood table lighter. Circa 1960's. 6¼" H., 3¼" Dia. at base. $10.00–20.00.

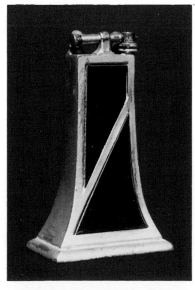

Plate 475 • "Tabourette" chromium and leather table lighter. Made by Ronson. Circa 1929. 4⅛" H., 2⅛" W. $110.00–150.00.

Plate 476 • Painted metal lift arm table lighter. Made by De-Lux. Circa 1928. 3⅞" H., 2¼" W. $55.00–70.00.

Plate 477 • Chromium table lighter made by Evans. Circa early 1930's. 3⅝" H., 2½" W. $25.00–40.00.

Plate 478 • Cylinder table lighters made by Daltis. Circa early 1930's. Both measure 4" H., 1⅜" Dia. at base. (a) Chromium. $35.00–50.00. (b) Goldplated. $60.00–70.00.

Plate 479 Chromium table lighter with leather covered base. Made by Thorens. Circa 1938. 3¾" H., 1¾" Dia. $60.00–80.00.

Plate 480 • Chromium and enamel table lighter. (Paint gets darker at the bottom.) Made by Evans. Circa 1934. 2⅜" H., 2¼" W. $25.00–40.00.

Plate 481 • "Corinthian" chromium table lighter made by Zippo. Circa 1960. 3⅞" H., 2¼" Dia. $35.00–50.00.

Plate 482 • Chromium and enamel table lighter. Circa late 1940's. 3¼" H., 1⅞" Dia. $25.00–40.00.

Plate 483 • Brass table lighter with floral and gold trim made by Evans. Circa late 1940's. 4⅞" H., 2¼" W. $45.00–60.00.

Plate 484 • Chromium ship wheel table lighter. (Lights by turning the wheel.) Made by Dunhill. Circa 1935. 5" H., 2⅞" Dia. at base. $175.00–250.00.

Plate 485 • "Nautical" touch tip table lighter with bronze finish and copper ship's wheel. Made by Ronson. Circa 1939. 4¾" H., 3" W. $225.00–300.00.

Plate 486 • Chromium cylinder table lighter made by Evans. Circa mid-1930's. 2¾" H., 1½" Dia. $30.00–45.00.

Plate 488 • Brass and plastic table lighter. Made by Jet Lighter Co. Circa early 1950's. 3" H., 1" Dia. $15.00–25.00.

Plate 489 • Brass table lighter made by Park Sherman. Circa early 1960's. 2½" H., 1½" W. $20.00–30.00.

Plate 487 • Brass and leather lift arm table lighter made in Japan by Nesor. Circa mid-1950's. 5¾" H., 3½" W. $40.00–60.00.

Plate 490 • Three-piece chromium table lighter set with plastic handles. Made by A.S.R. Circa early 1950's. Lighter, 3" H., 4¾" W. Cigarette holder, 2¼" H., 4¾" W. Tray, 5¾" x 9½". $75.00–90.00.

— MISCELLANEOUS ACCESSORIES —

Plate 491 • Brass lamp with ashtray at the base. (When the chain is pulled, the shade lowers to reveal a cigarette holder.) Circa 1950's. 8½" H., 4¼" W. $35.00–50.00.

Plate 492 • Brass-plated ship wheel cigarette holder. (Turn the wheel to raise cigarettes.) Circa mid-1950's. 5¼" H., 3⅞" Dia. at base. $30.00–40.00.

Plate 493 • Penciliters made by Havalite. Circa 1950. (a) Chromium and black plastic. 5⅝" H. (b) Chromium with black and white plastic. 5½" H. $30.00–40.00 each.

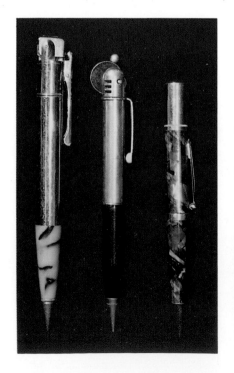

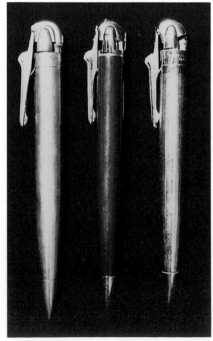

Plate 494 • Penciliters. (a) Chromium and Bakelite. Made in Occupied Japan. Circa 1949. 5½" H. $50.00– 70.00. (b) Metal and black plastic made by Automet. Circa 1950's. 5⅜" H. $20.00–30.00. (c) Chromium and jewel-tone plastic made by LECTRoLITE. Circa late 1940's. 5" H. $25.00–35.00.

Plate 495 • Penciliters made by Ronson. Circa 1949. All measured 5½" H. (a) Goldplated. $35.00–50.00. (b) Blue enamel. $40.00–65.00. (c) Silverplated. $35.00–50.00.

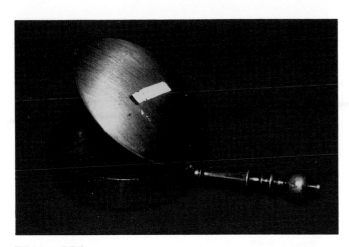

Plate 496 • Brass pocket ashtray with lit cigarette painted on the lid. Circa early 1950's. ½" H., 3" W. $20.00–30.00.

Plate 497 • Match safes. Circa 1900. Both measure 2¾" H., 1½" W. (a) Brass. $35.00–50.00. (b) Silverplated. $40.00–60.00.

Plate 498 • Old Gold cigarette tin with a place to strike matches on the bottom. Circa early 1930's. 3⅛" H., 2¼" W. $20.00–40.00.

Plate 499 • Match box and striker in the form of a book. Made of padded material over metal. Circa early 1960's. 2½" H., 2" W. $10.00–15.00.

Plate 500 • Matches in painted metal box by Enesco Imports Corp. Circa 1986. 1⅝" H., 2½" W. $5.00–10.00.

Plate 501 • Matches and box from Belgium. The box contains a built-in snuffer. (Matches are like candles and could be reused.) Circa 1900. 3½" H., 1½" W. $25.00–50.00.

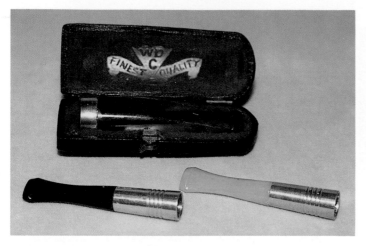

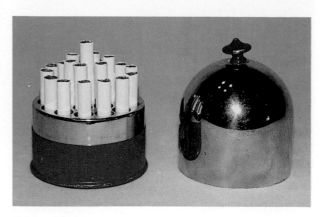

Plate 502 • (a) Cigar holder in leather and velvet case. Circa 1920's. 2¼" H., ½" Dia. $25.00–40.00. (b,c) Metal and plastic cigarette holders. Circa early 1950's. 2" H., ⅜" Dia. $10.00–15.00 each.

Plate 503 • Metal and enamel art deco cigarette holder. Circa late 1930's. 4½" H., 2⅞" Dia. $20.00–30.00.

Plate 504 • Package of Death Cigarettes from Holland. Circa 1993. 3⅜" H., 2⅛" W. $3.00–5.00.

Plate 505 • Lighter fluid tin for cigar lighters made by Enoz. Can had a cork stopper. Circa early 1920's. 3¾" H., 2¼" W. $20.00–30.00.

Plate 506 • Accessories by Ronson. (a) Package of flints, wicks, fuel, and brush. Circa late 1940's. 2" H., 1⅛" W. $10.00–15.00. (b) Package of five flints. Circa late 1940's. 1½" H., 1" W. $10.00–15.00.

Plate 507 • Matches from World War II. (a) Camp Carson, Colorado. 2" H., 3" W. (b) "Remember Pearl Harbor." 2" H., 1½" W. $5.00–10.00 each.

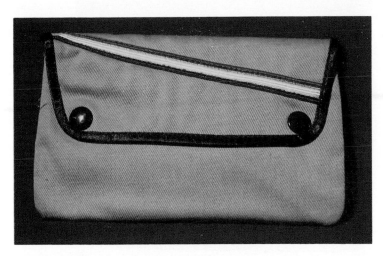

Plate 508 • Canvas tobacco pouch with red, white, and blue stripes on the flap. Circa World War II. 3¾" H., 6" W. $15.00–20.00.

Plate 509 • Metal ashtray from Ireland with an enamel shamrock in the center. Circa late 1940's. ½" H., 4¾" W. $25.00–35.00.

Plate 510 • Individual flint and wick packs on a cardboard display by Laymon's. Circa late 1930's. Display measures 11" H., 10½" W. $15.00–30.00.

Plate 511 • Wooden roll top cigarette box. Circa mid-1930's. 1⅞" H., 3⅜" W. $30.00–50.00.

Plate 512 • Silver matchbox covers. Both are circa late 1920's. (a) 1¾" H., 1¼" W. (b) 2¼" H., 1½" W. $15.00–25.00 each.

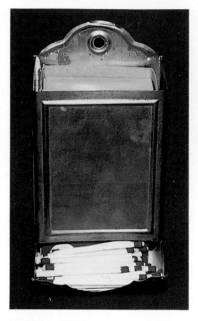

Plate 513 • Hanging tin match holder usually found by a stove. Circa early 1930's. 6" H., 3" W. $10.00–15.00.

Plate 514 • Tin "Sonny Boy" cigarette box from England. Circa mid-1920's. 3" H., 3⅜" W. $20.00–30.00.

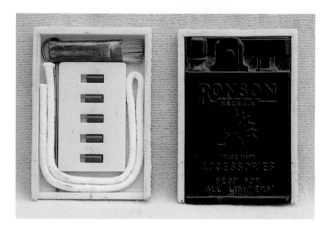

Plate 515 • Small plastic box with five flints, a wick, brush, and wick inserter. Made by Ronson. Circa late 1950's. 2" H., 1½" W. $10.00–15.00.

Plate 516 • Ceramic ashtray from Ireland. Circa mid-1950's. ¾" H., 4" W. $20.00–30.00.

Plate 517 • Chromium bird ashtray. Circa 1936. 2¼" H., 5¾" Dia. $20.00–35.00.

Plate 518, 519 • Walnut smoking stand. Circa mid-1930's. Note the inside compartment is lined with copper. 26" H., 17" W. $125.00–175.00.

— MAGAZINE ADVERTISEMENTS —

The following advertisements appeared from the mid-1930's to the late 1960's in *Life* and *Saturday Evening Post* magazines.

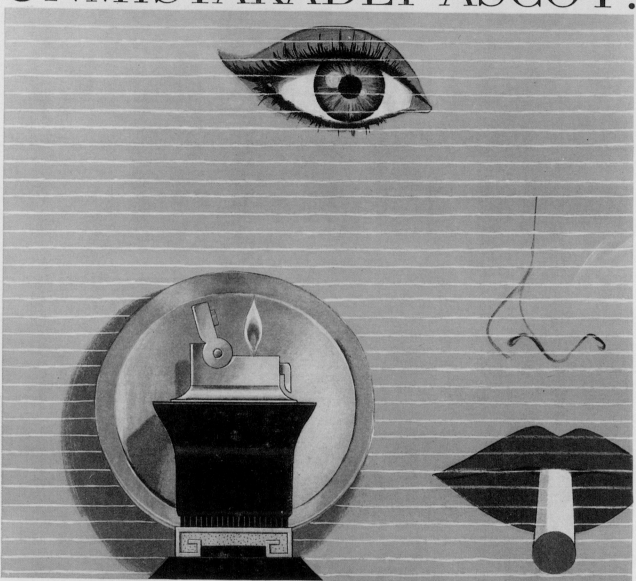
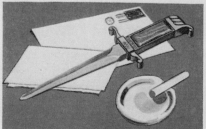

*so easy to choose . . .
so sure to please . . .
so proudly owned*

The "400" automatic lighter (b and c). No larger than a book of matches. World's thinnest, lightest, easiest to fill. Will not flood or leak. Easy to replace flint. Equalized flint pressure, sure-fire—patented—guaranteed.   Priced from $4⁹⁵

L'Élégant—a truly distinguished, tailored, engraved design in smart gold tone.

a. Cigarette Case. Holds king-size
   or regular $9⁹⁵
b. Lighter $7⁹⁵

Woodland Fawn—Any accessory of your choice in this superbly crafted design. The grace of each is accented in an engraved inlay effect in polished gold tone on satin silver.

c. Lighter $9⁹⁵
   Cigarette Case to match. Holds
   king-size or regular $9⁹⁵
d. Compact. Accommodates pressed
   or loose powder $9⁹⁵
e. Carryall—A treasured gift for milady.
   For all her vanity needs on any
   occasion. With carrying case . . . $17⁵⁰
   Also available with chain bracelet.
   Other styles in genuine alligator
   or bejeweled elegance from
   $12.95 to $35.00.

ELGIN AMERICAN
FASHION ACCESSORIES
REFLECT YOUR OWN GOOD TASTE

Compacts · Carryalls · Automatic Lighters · Cigarette Cases · Dresser Sets · Fashion Jewelry · Cultured and Simulated pearls. Cherished gifts on all occasions. Singly, each is a now and forever treasure—matched, the season's smartest gift ensemble.

**Light up the faces
under your Christmas Tree!**

Berkeley
WINDPROOF LIGHTERS

$2
INITIALS ENGRAVED 25c EXTRA

Sure-fire dependability in glowing Jeweltone colors or smart Silvertone finish . . . A fashion-right accessory that you'll be proud to give . . . proud to own.

For the extra-special names on your list: 24-K gold-plated inside and out
$4 (plus tax)

GUARANTEED FOR LIFE—unconditionally! Any damage repaired without charge, any time.

ONLY THE BERKELEY WINDPROOF LIGHTER HAS ALL THESE FEATURES

- **ASBESTOS WICK**—lasts for years.
- **ONE-PIECE FLAME GUARD**—nothing to break.
- **SECRET COMPARTMENT**—holds extra flint.
- **DOUBLE-SEALED — DOUBLY PROTECTED**—the inside mechanism is a complete lighter in itself—sealed at the bottom, to prevent fluid evaporation.

COPYRIGHT 1946, FLASHLIGHT CO. OF AMERICA, JERSEY CITY 2, N. J.

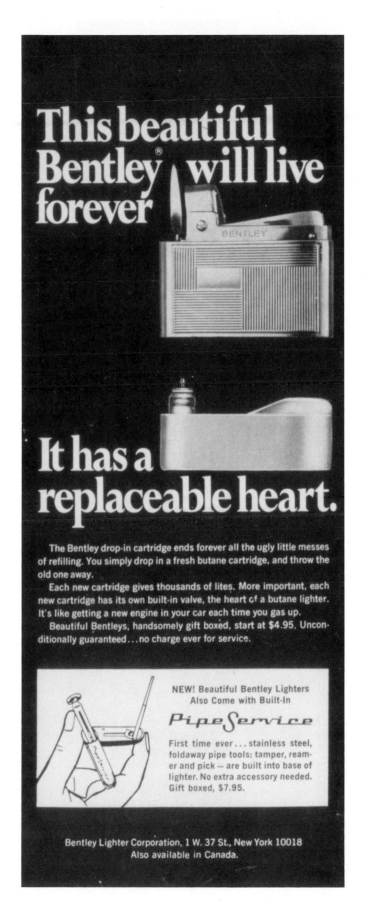

THE LIGHTER THAT MADE THE WORLD LIGHTER CONSCIOUS

*Above: Exquisitely engine turned 14K Gold $175.
Sterling Silver $20; plus 20% federal tax.*

Now on Hand

New windproof-beauty and matchless performance . . . backed by a tradition of functional excellence and a time honored life-time guarantee.

In giving a ZIPPO of gold or silver, you will be remembered continually, long after other quality gifts are forgotten. Prewar prices. Order early from your dealer, as supply is not abundant.

ZIPPO MFG. CO., Dept. X BRADFORD, PA.

Permanent wick, abundant fuel supply. Patented hinge-lock and assembly. "Sure spark" wheel. Life-time guaranteed, no one ever paid a cent to repair a ZIPPO.

Plain Sterling Silver case $15; 14K Gold $165, plus 20% federal tax.

Silverlike case $2.50, initials or facsimile of any signature $1.00 extra.

ZIPPO
WINDPROOF LIGHTER

WORLD'S MOST REVOLUTIONARY LITER!

New Models! New Features!

Ritepoint
VISIBLE FUEL LITERS

no finer liter to give
. . . or to get!

Remember Servicemen!

Pat. No. D-154,945. Other Pats. Pending

"see the fluid!"

$3.75
NO FED. TAX
and up

SIGNALS THE EYE
LONG BEFORE DRY!

TABLE DESK MODEL
$7.50
NO FED. TAX

Pat. No. D-159,281. Other Pats. Pending
Ritepoint Co. Exclusive Licensee

FUEL CONTROL! Just a few drops fill the wick chamber with exclusive Ritepoint patented fuel control!

SO EASY TO FILL Pull out spark wheel . . . unscrew seal plug, fill reservoir . . . in seconds!

At drug department gift and tobacco stores.

RITEPOINT CO. · ST. LOUIS (9) MO.

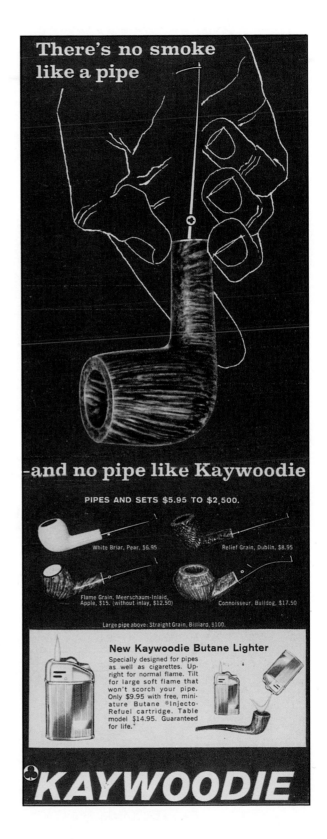

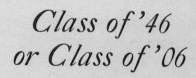

*Class of '46
or Class of '06*

Always studying, always increasing the breadth and depth of his knowledge—like this group watching a demonstration of a new method of using penicillin—the doctor's "school days" are never done. No matter how great, how famous he may become, his search for even greater knowledge never halts.

According to a recent Nationwide survey:

More Doctors smoke Camels than any other cigarette

Your "T-Zone" Will Tell You..

T for Taste . . .

T for Throat

. . . that's your proving ground for any cigarette. See if Camels don't suit your "T-Zone" to a "T."

R. J. Reynolds Tobacco Co.,
Winston-Salem, N. C.

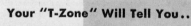

● Doctors in every branch of medicine—113,597 in all—were queried in this nationwide study of cigarette preference. Three leading research organizations made the survey. The gist of the query was—What cigarette do you smoke, Doctor?

The brand named most was Camel!

The rich, full flavor and cool mildness of Camel's superb blend of costlier tobaccos seem to have the same appeal to the smoking tastes of doctors as to millions of other smokers the world around. If you are a Camel smoker, this preference among doctors will hardly surprise you. If you're not—well, try Camels now.

CAMELS *Costlier Tobaccos*

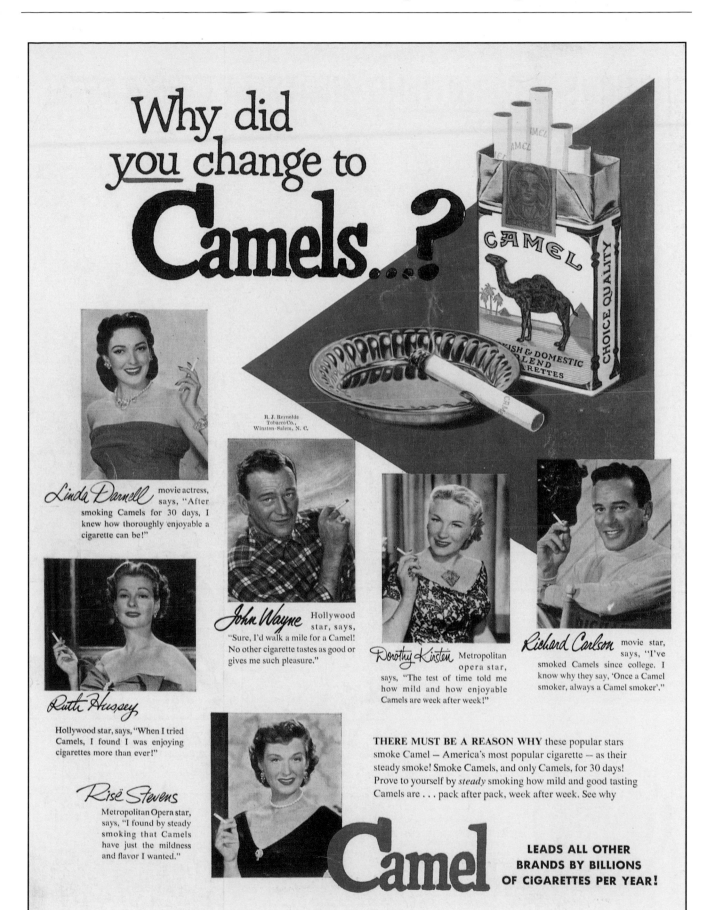

NOTHING—NO, NOTHING—BEATS BETTER TASTE!

and **LUCKIES TASTE** CLEANER, FRESHER, **BETTER!** SMOOTHER!

You can even see why Luckies taste better—cleaner, fresher, smoother

Ask yourself this question: *Why do I smoke?*

You know, yourself, you smoke for enjoyment. And you get enjoyment only from the taste of a cigarette.

Luckies taste better—cleaner, fresher, smoother! You can see *why* when you strip the paper from a Lucky by tearing down the seam.

First, you see that your Lucky is *made better*, because it remains a perfect cylinder of fine tobacco—round, firm and fully packed.

Second, you see Luckies' famous fine tobacco itself—long strands of fine, light, truly mild tobacco with a rich aroma and an even better taste. Yes, LS/MFT Lucky Strike *means* fine tobacco.

Nothing—no, nothing—beats better taste, and Luckies taste better—cleaner, fresher, smoother. So . . .

Be Happy—GO LUCKY!

PRODUCT OF *The American Tobacco Company* AMERICA'S LEADING MANUFACTURER OF CIGARETTES

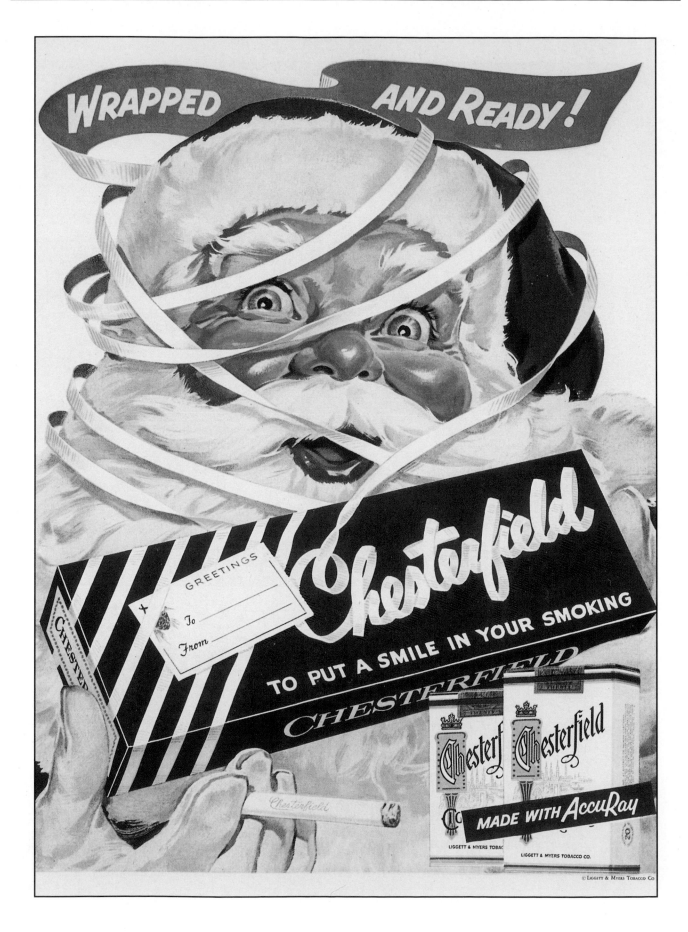

COLLECTOR BOOKS
Informing Today's Collector

DOLLS, FIGURES & TEDDY BEARS

2079	**Barbie** Doll Fashion, Volume I, Eames	$24.95
3957	**Barbie** Exclusives, Rana	$18.95
4557	**Barbie**, The First 30 Years, Deutsch	$24.95
3810	**Chatty Cathy** Dolls, Lewis	$15.95
4559	Collectible **Action Figures**, 2nd Ed., Manos	$17.95
1529	Collector's Encyclopedia of **Barbie** Dolls, DeWein/Ashabraner	$19.95
2211	Collector's Encyclopedia of **Madame Alexander Dolls**, 1965-1990, Smith	$24.95
4863	Collector's Encyclopedia of **Vogue Dolls**, Stover/Izen	$29.95
4861	Collector's Guide to **Tammy**, Sabulis/Weglewski	$18.95
3967	Collector's Guide to **Trolls**, Peterson	$19.95
1799	**Effanbee Dolls**, Smith	$19.95
5253	Story of **Barbie**, 2nd Ed., Westenhouser	$24.95
1513	**Teddy Bears & Steiff** Animals, Mandel	$9.95
1817	**Teddy Bears & Steiff** Animals, 2nd Series, Mandel	$19.95
2084	**Teddy Bears, Annalee's & Steiff** Animals, 3rd Series, Mandel	$19.95
1808	Wonder of **Barbie**, Manos	$9.95
1430	World of **Barbie** Dolls, Manos	$9.95
4880	World of **Raggedy Ann Collectibles**, Avery	$24.95

TOYS, MARBLES & CHRISTMAS COLLECTIBLES

3427	**Advertising Character** Collectibles, Dotz	$17.95
2333	Antique & Collectible **Marbles**, 3rd Ed., Grist	$9.95
4934	**Breyer Animal** Collector's Guide, Identification and Values, Browell	$19.95
4976	**Christmas** Ornaments, Lights & Decorations, Johnson	$24.95
4737	**Christmas** Ornaments, Lights & Decorations, Vol. II, Johnson	$24.95
4739	**Christmas** Ornaments, Lights & Decorations, Vol. III, Johnson	$24.95
2338	Collector's Encyclopedia of **Disneyana**, Longest, Stern	$24.95
4958	Collector's Guide to **Battery Toys**, Hultzman	$19.95
5038	Collector's Guide to **Diecast Toys** & Scale Models, 2nd Ed., Johnson	$19.95
4566	Collector's Guide to **Tootsietoys, 2nd Ed**, Richter	$19.95
3436	Grist's Big Book of **Marbles**	$19.95
3970	Grist's Machine-Made & Contemporary **Marbles**, 2nd Ed.	$9.95
5267	**Matchbox** Toys, 3rd Ed., 1947 to 1998, Johnson	$19.95
4871	**McDonald's Collectibles**, Henriques/DuVall	$19.95
1540	**Modern Toys** 1930–1980, Baker	$19.95
3888	**Motorcycle** Toys, Antique & Contemporary, Gentry/Downs	$18.95
5168	Schroeder's Collectible **Toys**, Antique to Modern Price Guide, 5th Ed	$17.95
1886	Stern's Guide to **Disney** Collectibles	$14.95
2139	Stern's Guide to **Disney** Collectibles, 2nd Series	$14.95
3975	Stern's Guide to **Disney** Collectibles, 3rd Series	$18.95
2028	**Toys**, Antique & Collectible, Longest	$14.95

JEWELRY, HATPINS, WATCHES & PURSES

1712	Antique & Collectible **Thimbles** & Accessories, Mathis	$19.95
1748	Antique **Purses**, Revised Second Ed., Holiner	$19.95
1278	Art Nouveau & Art Deco **Jewelry**, Baker	$9.95
4850	Collectible **Costume Jewelry**, Simonds	$24.95
3875	Collecting Antique **Stickpins**, Kerins	$16.95
3722	Collector's Ency. of **Compacts, Carryalls & Face Powder Boxes**, Mueller	$24.95
4940	**Costume Jewelry**, A Practical Handbook & Value Guide, Rezazadeh	$24.95
1716	Fifty Years of Collectible **Fashion Jewelry**, 1925-1975, Baker	$19.95
1424	**Hatpins** & Hatpin Holders, Baker	$9.95
1181	100 Years of Collectible **Jewelry**, 1850-1950, Baker	$9.95
3830	Vintage **Vanity Bags & Purses**, Gerson	$24.95

FURNITURE

1457	American **Oak** Furniture, McNerney	$9.95
3716	American **Oak** Furniture, Book II, McNerney	$12.95
1118	Antique **Oak** Furniture, Hill	$7.95
2132	Collector's Encyclopedia of **American** Furniture, Vol. I, Swedberg	$24.95
2271	Collector's Encyclopedia of **American** Furniture, Vol. II, Swedberg	$24.95
3720	Collector's Encyclopedia of **American** Furniture, Vol. III, Swedberg	$24.95
1755	Furniture of the **Depression Era**, Swedberg	$19.95
3906	**Heywood-Wakefield** Modern Furniture, Rouland	$18.95
1885	**Victorian** Furniture, Our American Heritage, McNerney	$9.95
3829	**Victorian** Furniture, Our American Heritage, Book II, McNerney	$9.95

INDIANS, GUNS, KNIVES, TOOLS, PRIMITIVES

1868	Antique **Tools**, Our American Heritage, McNerney	$9.95
1426	**Arrowheads** & Projectile Points, Hothem	$7.95
2279	**Indian** Artifacts of the Midwest, Hothem	$14.95
3885	**Indian** Artifacts of the Midwest, Book II, Hothem	$16.95
5162	**Modern Guns**, Identification & Values, 12th Ed., Quertermous	$12.95

2164	**Primitives**, Our American Heritage, McNerney	$9.95
1759	**Primitives**, Our American Heritage, Series II, McNerney	$14.95
4730	Standard **Knife** Collector's Guide, 3rd Ed., Ritchie & Stewart	$12.95

PAPER COLLECTIBLES & BOOKS

4633	**Big Little Books**, A Collector's Reference & Value Guide, Jacobs	$18.95
4710	Collector's Guide to **Children's Books**, 1850 to 1950, Jones	$18.95
1441	Collector's Guide to **Post Cards**, Wood	$9.95
2081	Guide to Collecting **Cookbooks**, Allen	$14.95
2080	Price Guide to **Cookbooks & Recipe Leaflets**, Dickinson	$9.95
3973	**Sheet Music** Reference & Price Guide, 2nd Ed., Pafik & Guiheen	$19.95
4654	**Victorian Trade Cards**, Historical Reference & Value Guide, Cheadle	$19.95
4733	**Whitman Juvenile Books**, Brown	$17.95

OTHER COLLECTIBLES

2269	Antique **Brass & Copper** Collectibles, Gaston	$16.95
1880	Antique **Iron**, McNerney	$9.95
3872	Antique **Tins**, Dodge	$24.95
1128	**Bottle** Pricing Guide, 3rd Ed., Cleveland	$7.95
3718	Collectible **Aluminum**, Grist	$16.95
4560	Collectible **Cats**, An Identification & Value Guide, Book II, Fyke	$19.95
4852	Collectible **Compact Disc** Price Guide 2, Cooper	$17.95
2018	Collector's Encyclopedia of **Granite Ware**, Greguire	$24.95
3430	Collector's Encyclopedia of **Granite Ware**, Book II, Greguire	$24.95
4705	Collector's Guide to Antique **Radios**, 4th Ed., Bunis	$18.95
4857	Collector's Guide to **Art Deco**, 2nd Ed., Gaston	$17.95
4933	Collector's Guide to **Bookends**, Identification & Values, Kuritzky	$19.95
3880	Collector's Guide to **Cigarette Lighters**, Flanagan	$17.95
4887	Collector's Guide to **Creek Chub Lures** & Collectibles, Smith	$24.95
3966	Collector's Guide to **Inkwells**, Identification & Values, Badders	$18.95
3881	Collector's Guide to **Novelty Radios**, Bunis/Breed	$18.95
4652	Collector's Guide to **Transistor Radios**, 2nd Ed., Bunis	$16.95
4864	Collector's Guide to **Wallace Nutting Pictures**, Ivankovich	$18.95
1629	**Doorstops**, Identification & Values, Bertoia	$9.95
3968	**Fishing Lure** Collectibles, Murphy/Edmisten	$24.95
5259	**Flea Market Trader**, 12th Ed., Huxford	$9.95
4945	**G-Men and FBI Toys**, Whitworth	$18.95
3819	**General Store Collectibles**, Wilson	$24.95
2216	**Kitchen Antiques**, 1790–1940, McNerney	$14.95
4950	The **Lone Ranger**, Collector's Reference & Value Guide, Felbinger	$18.95
2026	**Railroad** Collectibles, 4th Ed., Baker	$14.95
1632	**Salt & Pepper Shakers**, Guarnaccia	$9.95
5091	**Salt & Pepper Shakers** II, Guarnaccia	$18.95
2220	**Salt & Pepper Shakers** III, Guarnaccia	$14.95
3443	**Salt & Pepper Shakers** IV, Guarnaccia	$18.95
5007	**Silverplated Flatware**, Revised 4th Edition, Hagan	$18.95
1922	Standard **Old Bottle** Price Guide, Sellari	$14.95
3892	**Toy & Miniature Sewing Machines**, Thomas	$18.95
5144	Value Guide to **Advertising Memorabilia**, 2nd Ed., Summers	$19.95
3977	Value Guide to **Gas Station** Memorabilia, Summers	$24.95
4877	Vintage **Bar Ware**, Visakay	$24.95
4935	The W.F. Cody **Buffalo Bill** Collector's Guide with Values, Wojtowicz	$24.95
5281	**Wanted to Buy**, 7th Edition	$9.95

GLASSWARE & POTTERY

4929	**American Art Pottery**, 1880 – 1950, Sigafoose	$24.95
4938	Collector's Encyclopedia of **Depression Glass**, 13th Ed., Florence	$19.95
5040	Collector's Encyclopedia of **Fiesta**, 8th Ed., Huxford	$19.95
4946	Collector's Encyclopedia of **Howard Pierce Porcelain**, Dommel	$24.95
1358	Collector's Encyclopedia of **McCoy Pottery**, Huxford	$19.95
2339	Collector's Guide to **Shawnee Pottery**, Vanderbilt	$19.95
1523	Colors in **Cambridge Glass**, National Cambridge Society	$19.95
4714	**Czechoslovakian Glass** and Collectibles, Book II, Barta	$16.95
3725	**Fostoria**, Pressed, Blown & Hand Molded Shapes, Kerr	$24.95
4726	**Red Wing Art Pottery**, 1920s – 1960s, Dollen	$19.95

Schroeder's
ANTIQUES
Price Guide

. . . is the #1 best-selling antiques & collectibles value guide on the market today, and here's why . . .

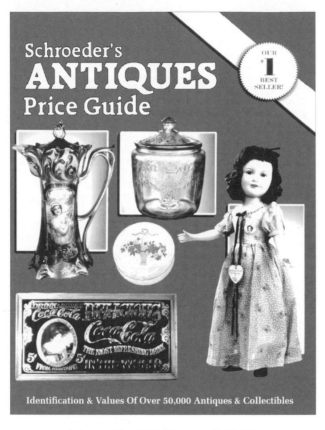

Schroeder's
ANTIQUES
Price Guide

OUR #1 BEST SELLER!

Identification & Values Of Over 50,000 Antiques & Collectibles

8½ x 11, 608 Pages, $12.95

• *More than 300 advisors, well-known dealers, and top-notch collectors work together with our editors to bring you accurate information regarding pricing and identification.*

• *More than 45,000 items in almost 500 categories are listed along with hundreds of sharp original photos that illustrate not only the rare and unusual, but the common, popular collectibles as well.*

• *Each large close-up shot shows important details clearly. Every subject is represented with histories and background information, a feature not found in any of our competitors' publications.*

• *Our editors keep abreast of newly developing trends, often adding several new categories a year as the need arises.*

If it merits the interest of today's collector, you'll find it in *Schroeder's*. And you can feel confident that the information we publish is up to date and accurate. Our advisors thoroughly check each category to spot inconsistencies, listings that may not be entirely reflective of market dealings, and lines too vague to be of merit. Only the best of the lot remains for publication.

Without doubt, you'll find
SCHROEDER'S ANTIQUES PRICE GUIDE
the only one to buy for
reliable information and values.

COLLECTOR BOOKS
A Division of Schroeder Publishing Co., Inc.